STRESS AND NEUROTIC BEHAVIOUR IN COLLEGE GIRLS

STRESS AND NEUROTIC BEHAVIOUR IN COLLEGE GIRLS

JANAK KUMARI SHRIVASTAVA

PUBLICATIONS

KALPAZ PUBLICATIONS

DELHI-110052

Stress and Neurotic Behaviour in College Girls

Rs. 720

ISBN: 81-7835-653-8

Published in 2008 in India by
Kalpaz Publications
C-30, Satyawati Nagar,
Delhi-110052
E-mail: kalpaz@hotmail.com
Phone : 9212729499

Lasser Type Setting by: Rudra Computer Graphics, Delhi
Printed at: Salasar Imaging System, Delhi

Dedicated to sacred memory of

"My beloved Father"

(Shri Rama Kant Lal Shrivastava)

Oh death! Where is thy Sting?

Contents

List of Tables 11

List of Figures 15

Foreword 17

Preface 19

Introduction 21

• Stress: Concept and Nature • Physical aspect of stress • Stress throughout evolution • The dynamics of stress • Sources of stress • Frustration • External Frustration • Internal Frustration • Conflict • Approach-avoidance conflicts • Double approach conflicts • Double avoidance conflicts • Pressure • Inner pressure • Outer pressure • Stress reaction: Physiological & Psychological • Stress can be positive • Understanding Neurotic Behaviour • Origin of Neuroses • Patterns of Neurotic Behaviour • General Symptoms • Psychopathy • Problems with relationships • Restricted development • Systematic effects • Specific syndromes • Anxiety reaction • Asthenic reaction • Conversion reaction • Dissociative reaction • Phobic Reaction • Obsessive-compulsive reaction • Neurotic depressive reaction • Suicide • Psychosomatic disorders • Hypochondriasis • Schizoid personality • Eating disoders • Dependency, addiction • Neurosis as disability • Manifest Neurotic symptoms • Concealed neurotic disorder • Career choice and neurotic behaviour • Social environment • Assessment of the disability • Vocational integration and neurotic Behaviour • Neurotics are not always failures • Summary chart of Psycho-neurotic disorder • Eysenck's two-dimensional framework

2. **Review of Literature** 71

• Stress: Nature • Drug abuse, Smoking and Stress • Life events, coping ability and Stress • Suicidal thoughts and Stress • Impact of performance on Stress • Post-traumatic Stress • Neurotic Behaviour : Concept • Studies related to neurotic behaviour • Present investigation: A word

3. **Methodology** 105

• Selection and formulation of problem • Objectives of the study • Hypotheses • Research Design • Measurement of Variables • Sample • Procedure • Plan of Analysis

4. **Analysis and Interpretation of Data** 127

• Analysis and interpretation • Different areas of stress • Sub-groups on the measures of stress • Curriculum and Stress • Level of education and Stress • Caste and Stress • Economic status and Stress • Different areas of Neurotic behaviour • Sub-groups on the measures of Neurotic behaviour • Curriculum and Neurotic behaviour • Level of education and Neurotic behaviour • Caste and Neurotic behaviour • Economic Status and Neurotic Behaviour • General Conclusions • Discriptive Findings • Key Findings.

5. **Summary and Conclusion** **197**
• Introduction • Objectives • Hypotheses • Sample • Measurement of Variables • Conclusions • Hypotheses-wise General Conclusions • Key Findings • Social Implications of the findings • Future Strategy • Limitations of the Present Study • Achievements: Suggestions to cope with stress in life • Contribution to Further Study

Bibliography **217**

Index **233**

List of Tables

3.1.	Description and Details of the Tools	108
3.2.	Dependibility, stability and internal consistency co-efficient of various stress scale.	112
3.3.	Distribution of items of scale of achievement stress.	114
3.4.	Distribution of items of scale of academic stress.	115
3.5.	Distribution of items of scale of physical stress.	116
3.6.	Distribution of items of scale of social stress.	117
3.7.	Distribution of items of scale of family stress.	118
3.8.	Distribution of items of Middlesex Hospital Questionnaire.	121
3.9.	Characteristics of the sample	123
4.1.	Student respondents and curriculum demographics	128
4.2.	Student respondents and level of education demographics	128
4.3.	Student respondents and caste demographics	129
4.4.	Student respondents and economic status demographics	129
4.5.	Comparison between arts and science sub-groups on achievement stress.	130

4.6.	Comparison between arts and science sub-groups on academic stress.	**131**
4.7.	Comparison between arts and science sub-groups on physical stress.	**133**
4.8.	Comparison between arts and science sub-groups on social stress.	**134**
4.9.	Comparison between arts and science sub-groups on family stress.	**136**
4.10.	Comparison between arts and science sub-groups on total stress.	**137**
4.11.	Comparison between post-graduate and under-graduate sub-groups on achievement stress.	**139**
4.12.	Comparison between post-graduate and under-graduate sub-groups on academic stress.	**140**
4.13.	Comparison between post-graduate and under-graduate sub-groups on physical stress.	**142**
4.14.	Comparison between post-graduate and under-graduate sub-groups on social stress.	**143**
4.15.	Comparison between post-graduate and under-graduate sub-groups on family stress.	**144**
4.16.	Comparison between post-graduate and under-graduate sub-groups on total stress.	**146**
4.17.	Comparison between upper caste and lower caste sub-groups on achievement stress.	**149**
4.18.	Comparison between upper caste and lower caste sub-groups on academic stress.	**150**
4.19.	Comparison between upper caste and lower caste sub-groups on physical stress.	**151**
4.20.	Comparison between upper caste and lower caste sub-groups on social stress.	**154**
4.21.	Comparison between upper caste and lower caste sub-groups on family stress.	**155**

4.22. Comparison between upper caste and lower caste sub-groups on total stress. **157**

4.23. Mean scores of three groups viz; high, middle and low economic level female college students on Bisht Battery of Stress Scale. **158**

4.24. Results of ANOVA showing differences between three groups viz; high, middle and low economic sub-groups on achievement stress. **159**

4.25. Results of ANOVA showing differences between three groups viz; high, middle and low economic sub-groups on academic stress. **160**

4.26. Results of ANOVA showing differences between three groups viz; high, middle and low economic sub-groups on physical stress. **161**

4.27. Results of ANOVA showing differences between three groups viz; high, middle and low economic sub-groups on social stress. **162**

4.28. Results of ANOVA showing differences between three groups viz; high, middle and low economic sub-groups on family stress. **164**

4.29. Results of ANOVA showing differences between three groups viz; high, middle and low economic sub-groups on total stress. **165**

4.30. Comparison between arts and science sub-groups on MHQ and its different aspects. **170**

4.31. Comparison between post-graduate and under-graduate sub-groups on MHQ and its different aspects. **174**

4.32. Comparison between upper caste and lower caste sub-groups on MHQ and its different aspects. **176**

4.33. Mean scores of three groups viz; high, middle, and low economic level female college girls on MHQ and its different aspects. **179**

4.34. Results of ANOVA showing differences between three groups viz; high, middle and low economic sub-groups on MHQ and its different aspects. **181**

List of Figures

Fig. 1	Hypothetical relationships between concepts, Yorklea Social Environmental Survey(1968)	**34**
Fig. 2	Hierarchy of Stress-Distress Indicators, Yorklea Social Environmen t Survey	**34**
Fig. 3	The effects of stress, illness and preventive action as seen in chain reaction	**41**
Fig. 4	Eysenck's two-dimensional framework	**69**
Fig. 5	A comparative picture of arts and science sample groups on various aspects of Bisht Battery of Stress Scale, as a whole.	**135**
Fig. 6	An account of the global picture of post-graduate and under-graduate sample groups on various aspects of Bisht Battery of Stress Scale, as a whole.	**147**
Fig. 7	A graphic representation of arts and science; under-graduate and post-graduate sample groups on various combinations.	**147**
Fig. 8	A quick glance of the outcome of upper caste and lower caste sample groups on various aspects of Bisht Battery of Stress Scale, as a whole.	**153**
Fig. 9	A graphic representation of high, middle and low economic level sample groups on BBSS and its different aspects.	**163**

Fig. 10	A quick glance of arts and science; high, middle and low economic level sample groups on BBSS and its different aspects.	**167**
Fig. 11	A quick glance of the outcome as a whole on various aspects of BBSS in various combination.	**168**
Fig. 12	A comparative picture of arts and science sample groups on various aspects of Middlesex Hospital Questionnaire, as a whole.	**172**
Fig. 13	An account of the global picture of post-graduate and under-graduate sample groups on various aspects of Middlesex Hospital Questionnaire, as a whole.	**175**
Fig. 14	A graphic representation of arts and science; under-graduate and post-graduate sample groups on various aspects of Middlesex Hospital Questionnaire, as a whole.	**176**
Fig. 15	A quick glance of the outcome of upper caste and lower caste sample groups on various aspects of Middlesex Hospital Questionnaire, as a whole.	**178**
Fig. 16	A comparative picture of high, middle and low economic level sample groups on various aspects of Middlesex Hospital Questionnaire, as a whole.	**180**
Fig. 17	A graphic representation of arts and science; high, middle and low economic status sample groups in various combinations.	**183**
Fig. 18	A quick glance of the outcome as a whole on various aspects of Middlesex Hospital Questionnaire, as a whole.	**184**

Foreword

Stress is the product of modern life style, all over the world. Stress causes physiological and psychological changes in individuals. Disturbances in the structure or function of bodily mechanisms and cognitive spheres may be brought through creating change in physical or psychological environment. Stress, in fact is the outcome of the demands made on an individual beyond the capacity of his potentials to cope with the situation. Stress and coping both, therefore, go side by side. Ability to cope with a task dealing with a situation is inversely related to the degree of stress. Mediating role of cognitive process in psychological stress is well known yet the relationship between the cognitive process, adaptive behaviour and psychological outcome is not very clear. Role of individual is very dominant in perception of 'good' stressors such as commitment to accomplishment and 'bad' stressors such as resentment and frustration. Personality plays an important role in such a perception. Threatening stimuli sometimes are perceived as positive one. Individual with such an attitude is actually involved in self deception using defense mechanism such as self denial or reaction formation. These defenses indicate the concealment of conflicting inner states and require considerable adaptatimal capacity. Further anger, fear and anxiety, important emotional states, contribute differently to reaction to stress which may vary to a great extent from positive viz; elation to negative viz; despair ones.

Frustrating situations normally elicits anger, danger is elicited by fear and threat leads to anxiety often leads to the development of abnormal behaviour. The author in the present book has attempted to study some such problems in college girls adapting scientific methodology. The findings of study are meaningful. The findings have both academic as well as applied value. This will be of great help to psychologists, research workers, policy makers, planners, parents and executives.

Prof. G. P. Thakur
Former President
Indian Academy of Applied Psychology

Preface

With advancement in civilization and modernization individuals' life has become more complex resulting in stress and neurotic behaviour. Stress and neurotic behaviour of college life is a significant factor for individual's proper growth. College students in the transition period between late adolescence and early adulthood have may special stresses with which they must contend exams, grades, sex and pressure from parents creates high level of stress and poor mental health. Investigation, therefore, on the issue of stress and neurotic behaviour needed special attention in the Indian context. Incidence of stress and neurotic behaviour is not known in India particularly in student population, therefore, it was felt the need of the hour to ascertain the incidence and quality of stress as well as neurotic behaviour in college girls.

The subject matter of the present book has been split into five chapters. The first chapter deals with the introduction, second chapter is devoted to the review of literature, the third chapter throws the light on the statement of the problem and methodology, the fourth chapter deals with the results and discussion and the fifth chapter as well as the last chapter deals with summary and conclusions. The references are given at the end of the book.

My sincere graitudes to Late Prof. T.S. Dhapola and Prof. G.P. Thakur, Department of Psychology, Mahatma Gandhi Kashi Vidyapeeth University Varanasi (U.P.) for their kind inspiration, supervision and active support.

A special note of profound indebtedness is due to Dr. Swarn Singh, Joint Director (Physical), Anthropological Survey of India. I am deeply indebted and express my whole hearted regards to him, for his constant encouragement, inspiration, and interest.

I take this opportunity to express my profound regards to Late Prof. (Smt.) Manju Thakur, Department of Psychology, B. B. A. Bihar University, for ecouragement and support.

I shall be failing in my duty if I do not express my thanks to the students who participated as subjects for their interest, co-operation and willingness. Without whose co-operation this work could not be possible.

I am unable to express my deep feeling for my beloved mother Smt. Kamala Shrivastava, acknowledging her affection seems too formal. I am in fact indebted to her. A deep sense of affection I also express to my sisters (Usha & Ohm) and brothers (Nirankar Swaroop & Brahma Swaroop) who helped in many odd and even moments, with whom I share my genes.I express my deep affection to my nieces Purty, Iti and Suhani for their unconditional love for me, which is always give me extra energy.

Sri Debasis Biswas of Anthropological Survey of India needs special mention for getting the manuscript ready in presentable form

The 26th November, 2007
Janak Kumari Shrivastava

Introduction

Of all the time in history man has been suffering more stress and strain today. The new techno-economic advancements have resulted into a tempo of life with which it is difficult to cope for the modern man. If we can put the matter metaphorically man has now become the victim of the monster of progress created by himself. The modern civilization has exacted a heavy price from man in the form of greater stress and more painful strain than ever in human history.

Modern civilization has made man's life more convenient by providing various facilities with the help of scientific invention. On the contrary, too much automation has made them victims of unemployment and dislocation. Excessive competition, conflicting pressures of groups, rapid social changes, racial discriminations, feelings of frustrations, hatred and resentment aggravate modern man's anxieties, stresses and his ailments . Everywhere we see worried, unhappy people, who are unable to utilize their best potentialities, because of their unsatisfactory adjustment to their environment. Instead of smooth, effective functioning we find widespread symptoms of personality maladjustment. There have been profound changes in our society since the 1950s, characterised by a sharp increase in stress levels. Job security has all but disappeared, as we experience pressure to be 'flexible' in our work. One section of the population is unemployed, while another is overworked. An increased emphasis on competitiveness in work and society has meant that we are constantly experiencing assessment, comparison, devolution and disparagement. The ever-expending power of global corporations has led to a feeling of helplessness. People are far more mobile than earlier times– they no longer expect to spend their lives in the community in which they were born, and thus no longer have the daily support of their extended family and community. The nature of the family has changed, with the growth of one-parent, step and grandparent families. But perhaps the most dramatic development has been in information technology. We are constantly bombarded with information – from radio, television, mobile phones, advertisement and internate. Even a modern car of multitude signals force themselves on the driver's attention. All these lead to sensory overload, which in turn lead to develop stress, which is a major contributory factor in mental illness. In many cases, the stress of modern life proves too much for an individual to cope with, and he/she suffers a psychiatric or psychosomatic casualty.

The term 'psychosomatic' is used in two senses: (1) psychosomatic approach to the medicine, (2) psychosomatic disorder. It would be desirable to deal with psychosomatic approach to the medicine first. This concept is as old as medicine itself. Evil spirits supposed to enter the body and cause the diseases. The treatment was obviously to remove evil spirits by *exorcisms or trephining* of the skull. The *Atharva Veda* is full of '*charms*' and '*mantras*' used for the purpose. The *Atharva Vaidic Jeevak* as a personal physician of lord Buddha, used to trephine the skull and bring out worms from head, thus effectively to cure the patients. This appears to have taken place in 500 B.C. Similarly, from 2500 to 500 B.C., when Babilonian, Assurian and the Indus Valley civilization flourished, medicine was dominated by religion. Suggestion was the major tool for recovery. The *Shastras* may be said to have anticipated the psychotherapy of the 19th and 20th centuries. He suggests that 'passions and strong emotions might cause not only mental disease but might even be responsible for certain physical conditions which require the help of surgery' (Zilboorg and Henry, 1941). During 500 B.C. Greek civilization dominated the world when *Socrates* said, 'not be cured the eyes without the head, not head without body, so neither it is proper to cure the body without soul.'

During 16th, 17th and 18th centuries interest in science was revived. Leeuwenhoek (Anton Van Leeuwenhoek 1632 - 1723) discovered microscope with the result that mind was relegated to philosophy and religion. Virchow (Rudolf Virchow 1821 - 1902) appeared in the same period, during 19th and 20th centuries and established that 'disease has its origin in disease of the cells'. Man was conceived of as a machine, who was made up of different organs. Just as machine requires repair of its parts, similarly each organ has to be treated and repaired.

Stress : Concept and Nature

The concept of stress and its effect upon victims is an ancient one. The word 'stress' itself is an abbreviation of the original term 'distress'. It has come to modern usage through old French and middle English. The stress is external to the organism and the effects occurring within the organism are to be collectively termed strain.

The word 'stress' is defined by the Oxford Dictionary as 'a state of affair involving demand on physical or mental energy'. A condition or circumstance (not always adverse), which can disturb the normal physical and mental health of an individual. In medical parlance 'stress,' is defined as a perturbation of the body's homeostasis. This demand on mind-body occurs when it tries to cope with incessant changes in life. A 'stress' condition seems 'relative' in nature. Extreme stress conditions, psychologists say, are detrimental to human health but in moderation stress is normal and, in many cases, proves useful. Stress, nonetheless, is synonymous with negative conditions. Today, with the rapid diversification of human activity, we come face to face with numerous causes of stress and the symptom of stress and depression.

At one point or the other, everybody suffers from stress. Relationship demands, physical as well as mental health problems, pressure at workplaces, traffic snarls, meeting deadlines, growing-up tensions-all of these conditions and situations are valid causes of stress. People have their own methods of stress management. In some people, stress induced adverse feelings and anxieties tend to persist and intensify. Learning to understand and master stress management techniques can help prevent the counter effects of this urban malaise.

In a critical review (Eastham, Coates, & Allodi, 1970), it is noted that the terms 'stress' and 'crisis' were used interchangeably by investigators and with reference to markedly different experiences; for instance, those of individuals and families and those of face-to-face groups, organizations and communities. By contrast, our models emphasized differences between stress experienced in isolation and in a context of mutual support, as well as between stressful events for which culturally prescribed modes of response existed and events for which anticipation was impossible. To adequately deal with these complexities, Coates, Moyer, Kendall & Howat (1976) developed several models for empirical testing.

Stress is commonly viewed as a frustrated 'fight or flight' response a basic human survival mechanism left over from our primordial 'roots' when we could best respond to perceived dangers by either fighting or fleeing; seen in this way, stress behaviour and emotions are sometimes regarded as problematic inappropriate responses to threatening situations in modern civilize society, however, stress is a) a powerful internal communication to raise awareness, and b) a source of energy; although the raw emotional and physical energies may have to be transformed into a more useful form before they are directly useful.

The term 'stress' has been used so loosely, and so many confusing definitions of it have been formulated, according to Hans Selye (1957) it will be most instructive to start out by stating clearly what it is not. Contrary to this are some current but vague or misleading statements:

1. *Stress is not nervous tension* **:** Stress-reactions do occur in lower animals which have no nervous system. An alarm reaction can be induced by mechanically damaging an enervated limb. Indeed, stress can be produced in cell cultures grown outside of the body.
2. *Stress is not an emergency discharge of hormones from the adrenal medulla* **:** An adrenaline-discharge is frequently seen in acute stress affecting the whole body, but it plays no conspicuous role in generalized inflammatory disease (arthritis, tuberculosis), although they can also produce considerable stress; nor does it play any role in local stress-reactions limited to directly injured territories of the body.
3. *Stress is not anything that causes a secretion, by the adrenal cortex, of its hormones, the corticoids :* ACTH, the adrenal-stimulating pituitary hormone, can discharge corticoids without producing any evidence of stress.
4. *Stress is not the non-specific result of damage :* Normal activities – a game of tennis or even a passionate kiss can produce considerable stress without causing conspicuous damage.
5. *Stress is not any deviation from homeostasis, the steady state of the body*: Any biologic function (the perception of

sound or light, the contraction of a muscle) causes marked deviations from the normal resting state in the active organs.

6. *Stress is not anything that causes an alarm reaction* : It is the stressor that does that, not stress itself.
7. *Stress is not identical with the alarm reaction of the G.A.S. (general adaptation syndrome) as a whole* : These reactions are characterised by certain measurable organ-changes which are caused by stress and hence could not themselves be stress.
8. *Stress is not a non-specific reaction* : The pattern of the stress-reaction is very specific. It affects certain organs (for instance, the adrenal, the thymus, the gastrointestinal tract) in highly selective manner.
9. *Stress is not a specific reaction* : The stress-response is, by definition, not specific, since it can be produced by virtually any agent

The more precise definition of stress is as follows- 'Stress is the state manifested by a specific syndrome, which consists of all the non-specifically induced changes within a biologic system'. Thus stress has its own characteristic form and composition but no particular cause. The elements of it's form are the visible changes due to stress, whatever be its cause. They are addictive indicators which can express the sum of all the different adjustments that are going on the body at any time. This is essentially an 'operational definition'; which tells what must be done to produce and recognize stress. A state can be recognized only by its manifestation; for example, the state of stress by the manifestations of the stress syndrome. Therefore, one has to observe a great many living beings exposed to a variety of agents before one can see the shape and stress as such. Thus, stress is a state manifested by syndrome. Stress shows itself as a specific syndrome, yet it is non-specifically induced. According to Hans Selye (1957) 'stress is the sum of all non-specific changes caused by function or damage.'

A simple practical definition of stress is the uncomfortable gap between (a) how we could like our life to be and (b) how it actually is, if this gap is persistent (or even worse: growing!)-despite our efforts to reduce it, our distress is particularly acute. Stress is a medical term for a wide range of strong external stimuli, both physiological and psychological, which can cause a physiological response called the general adaptation syndrome, first described by Hans Selye in the Journal Nature.

The intensity of the internally distributed forces or components of forces that resist a change in the volume or shape of material. That has been subjected to external forces. Stress is expressed in force per unit area and is calculated on the basis of original dimensions of cross section of the specimen. Stress can be either direct (tension or compression) or shear. The sum of the biological reactions to any adverse stimulus-physical, mental or emotional, internal or external, that tends to disturb a person's normal state of well-being. An emotionally disruptive or upsetting condition occurring in response to adverse external influences and capable of effecting physical health which can be characterised by increased heart rate, a rise in blood pressure, muscular tension, irritability and depression. Stress does not cause migraine but can be a migraine 'trigger'. Any real or perceived adverse stimuli, physical or psychological, that tends to disturb an individual's homeostasis. A condition in which the organism is subjected to unfavourable or unfamiliar environmental conditions, resulting in some alteration in normal physical functioning. Short-term stress can often be overcome but long-term stress can reduce resistance to disease and parasites, inhibit self-healing processes, and reduce life-span.

Stress is a 'particular pattern of disturbing psychological and physiological reactions that occur when an environmental event threatens important motives and taxes one's ability to cope'. In general English, stress is the 'wear and tear' our bodies experience as we adjust to our continually changing environment. But all stresses are not bad-some stress is good .In fact, everyone needs stress in their lives; without it, life would be dull and unexciting. Stress adds flavour, challenge and opportunity to life. Stress can pump up, give energy, supply that zest for living.

Stress is an avoidable part of life. The challenge caused by stress help to develop new skills and behaviour patterns. The problems occur, however, when stress becomes excessive. It can become destructive and can turn into distress. Too much stress on our mind and body can make us feel miserable, worried, sad and ill. Contrary to popular belief, stress is not the pressure from the outside-the divorce, the death, the burned supper, the vacation, the isolation. Those are stressors. Our response to those situations constitutes stress. Stress is a part of our lives. It is especially likely to happen when we are experiencing changes-either happy or upsetting changes. One may be feeling a lot of stress, when-

- Experiencing- or facing—a change in environment.
- Physical development is behind or ahead.
- There are problems at home: parents fighting, an alcoholic parent, a serious illness in the family, money worries, a parental separation or divorce, psychological or physical abuse from a parent or sibling.
- Someone close died —a grandparent, parent or other close relative, a special friend, or a pet.
- Everyone seems to expect a lot.

There are number of different results from stress. These results include stomach aches and diarrhoea, for example, before exams or a much anticipated date or rather major event. Although some people may not be affected a great deal by stress, other people have chronic problems such as irritable bowel syndrome or colitis, or diarrhoea and constipation. Some symptoms are as follows-

- increased heart rate
- rapid breathing
- stammering
- headaches, stomach aches, chest pain
- diarrhoea
- sweating
- sleeplessness
- alcohol and drug addiction

These stress symptoms are not to be feared, but they do signal that we are not managing our life effectively. They indicate that changes need to be made sooner or later, or more nervous consequences may follow.

Life is fine running thread interrupted by beads of stresses that are integral to living. The term 'stress' has been widely and indiscriminately used; its most precise definition is that of Selye (1950). He restricts the concept of stress to a characteristic psychological response differentiating this from 'stressors' – the agents which produce stress. Hans Selye (1950) has rightly put it 'life without stress is death'. Stress offers opportunities not only for growth, development and maturity; but they can also serve as pathogens and we have a pageantry of stress disorders. This bodily reaction is manifested through the symptoms of a general adaptation syndrome typically including three stages : (a) an alram reaction, including an initial shock phase, in which defensive mechanisms begin to operate; (b) a stage of resistance in which adaptation is optimal; and (c) a stage of exhaustion, marked by the collapse of the adaptive response.

The features of this reaction are organized around the pituitary - adrenal cortical axis. Selye describes the trial of alarm reaction as enlargement of the adrenals shrinkage of the thymus and lymples nodes, and gastro-intestial ulceration.

A sympathetic nervous system or adrenal medulla stress reactions (Cannon, 1932), was made within the concept of systematic euqilibration. The general effect of the stress syndrome appears to be the modifications of bodily processes so as to make available the energy resources normally kept in reserve or used for other functions such as digestion or anabolism (Cofer & Apply, 1964)

Physical Aspects of Stress

Neurotransmitters send and receive messages between brain cells. There are two kinds of messengers- 'happy' messenger (cheerful and enthusiastic messages) and 'sad' messenger (cheerless and silencing messages). Too much stress causes the happy messengers to eventually begin to fail. Sad messages overtake happy ones, causing a chemical imbalance. This chemical imbalance is overstress. Everyone experiences short durations of overstress.

The three 'happy' messengers are-Serotonin, Noradrenalin, and Dopamine.

Our body clock is located in a supply of Serotonin in the Pineal Gland in the brain. Our body clock coordinates our body functions to the same rhythm. For example, it sets our physiology for sleeping and waking-up. Our body clock also controls the secretion of the chief stress fighting hormone Cortisol.Disruption of our cortisol cycle makes sleeping more difficult. Serotonin is often the first happy messenger to malfunction under stress. Thus, lack of restful sleep is usually the first symptom of overstress.

Noradrenalin sets our energy levels, and makes us feel energized. Failure of this happy messenger causes overstressed people to feel as though they don't have the energy to do much of anything.

Dopamine is located adjacent to where Endorphin is released in the brain and so there is a link, so that when Dopamine function declines, so does Endorphin function.

Endorphins regulate pain and so, pain increases when stress causes the Dopamine function to fail.

Dopamine also operates our pleasure centre. Thus, when stress incurs on our Dopamine function, it can also result in a loss of pleasure in normally pleasureful affairs.

Our stress tolerance determines the amount of stress we can handle before our happy messengers begin to fail. Stress tolerance is hereditary. It is observed that ten per cent of our population has inherited low stress tolerance. This means one out of ten persons feel overly stressed all of the time.

Those, who experience overstress sometimes use substances to temporarily make feel better. Some of these substances which can restore balance by chemically boosting the happy messengers are-

- Sugar
- Caffeine
- Alcohol
- Solvents
- Drugs
- Tobacco
- Adrenalin

However, these happy messenger boosters don't work well. They do not maintain balance between the stressors and boosters. This leads to a roller-coaster of good and bad feelings.

First of all, the minute changes in chemical levels can not accurately be adjusted by consuming happy messenger boosters.

Secondally, these boosters cause a roller coaster to start. After our happy messengers are temporarily boosted, we experience a fall. The higher the boost, the greater the fall.

Finally, another problem with happy messenger boosters is that our body adapts to them quickly. Once they are adapted to, the more of them we will need to experience the desired effect.

Side effects of boosters worsen the problem of overstress-

- Sugar high lead to sugar lows. Too much sugar worsen overstress.
- Alcohol can cause liver failure and bleeding complications, as well as a greater risk of violence and fatal traffic accidents. Alcohol worsen overstress.
- Tobacco can damage lungs and arteries, and may cause cancer. Tobacco worsen overstress.
- Caffeine can cause abnormal heart rhythms. Caffeine worsen overstress.
- Illegal drugs can cause convulsions, overdoes, even death. Illegal drugs worsen overstress.

Prescriptive medicines intended to force the body into sleeping or tranquilizing, such as valium, can also worsen stress. They keep our body from restoring its happy messengers. If taken for long periods of time, these medicines will have severe withdrawal syndrome.

Stress Throughout Evolution

Stress has existed throughout the evolution. About four billion years ago, violent collision of rock and ice along with dust and gas, led to the formation of a new planet. The planet survive 100 million years of meltdown to give birth; to microscopic life . These first organisms endured the harshest conditions-lack of oxygen, exposure to sun's UV (ultraviolet) rays and other inhospitable elements, to hang on to their dear life. Roughly, 300,000 years ago, the Neanderthals learnt to use fire in a controlled way, to survive the Glacial Age. In addition, around 30,000 years ago, Homo sapiens with their dominant gene constitutions and better coping skills, won the game of survival. Each step of evolution a test of survival, and survival, a matter of coping with the stress of changing conditions.

Millions of trials and errors in the life process have brought men to this stage. Coping with events to survive has led men to invent extraordinary technologies, beginning with a piece of sharpened stone.

From the viewpoint of micro-evolution, stress induction of transpositions is a powerful factor, generating new genetic variations in populations under stressful environmental conditions. Passing through a 'bottleneck', a population can rapidly and significantly alter its population norm and become the founder of new, evolved forms.

Gene transposition through Transposable Elements (TE)-'jumping genes', is a major source of genetic change, including the creation of novel genes, the alteration of gene expression in development, and the genesis of major genomic rearrangements. In a research on 'the significance of responses of the genome to challenges,' the Nobel Laureate Barbara McClintock, characterized these genetic phenomena as 'genomic shock'. This occurs due to recombination events between TE insertions (high and low insertion polymorphism) and host genome. But, as a rule TEs remain immobilized until some stress factor (temperature, irradiation, DNA damage, the introduction of foreign chromatin, viruses, etc.) activates their elements.

The moral remains that we can work a stress condition to our advantage or protect ourselves from its untoward follow-throughs subject to how we handle a stress situation. The choice is between becoming a slave to the stressful situations of life or using them to our advantage.

The model emphasises the centrality of current experience, which is conditioned by both past experience and current events (occurrences), and in turn it affects both current subjective state (mental health or distress) and overt help-seeking behaviour. Since this model was too global for empirical testing, it gave rise to a second model (Fig.2), which predicted

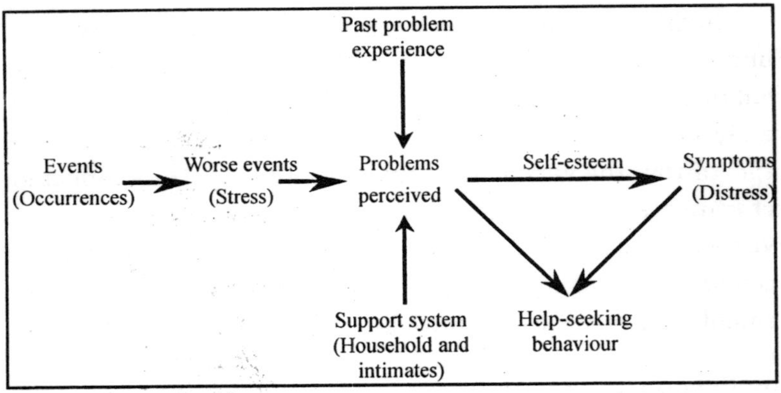

Fig. 1. Hypothetical relationships between concepts, *Yorklea Social Environment Survey* (1968).

Source : Coates, D.B. Yorklea Social Environment Survey. (Tech. Rep.) Tornoto: Clarke Institute of Psychiatry, 1970: cited for research purpose.

the direction and intensity of relationships between alternative indicators for many of the concepts cited. the use of multiple indicators for stress and distress and for categorising the social environment has created difficulties in analysing and presenting the results.

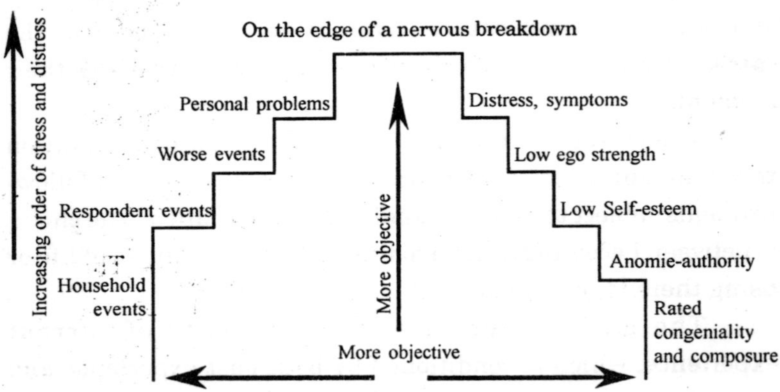

Fig. 2. Hierarchy of Stress-Distress Indicators, *Yorklea Social Environment Survey* (1968).

Source: Coates, D.B. Yorklea Social Environment Survey. (Tech. Rep.) Tornoto : Clarke Institute of Psychiatry, 1970 : cited for research purpose.

In this phase, the family as a dynamic unit was the subject of inquiry; thus, each component was re-examined in terms of available survey data about sources of chronically stressful family or household situations. Furthermore, it seemed important to consider the cumulative effects of multiple stressful situations, in addition to the chronicity of each one, which necessitated developing unduplicated counts. Above all, one wanted to make sure that each component did not include elements of the dependent variables one would try to predict.

The Dynamics of Stress

'Nothing gives one person so much advantage over another as to remain always cool and unruffled under all circumstances' -Thomas Jefferson.

In a challenging situation the brain prepares the body for defensive action – the fight or flight response by releasing stress hormones, namely, cortisone and adrenaline. These hormones raise the blood pressure and the body prepares to react to the situation. With a concrete defensive action, (fight response) the stress hormones in the blood get used up, entailing reduced stress effects and symptoms of anxiety. When we fail to counter a stress situation, (flight response) the hormones and chemicals remain unreleased in the blood stream for a long period. It results in stress related physical symptoms such as tense muscles, unfocused anxiety, dizziness and rapid heartbeats. We all encounter various stressors (causes of stress) in everyday life, which can accumulate, if not released. Subsequently, it compels the mind and body to be in an almost constant alarm-state in preparation to fight or flee. This state of accumulated stress can increase the risk of both acute and chronic psychosomatic illnesses and weaken the immune system of the human body.

Stress can cause headaches, irritable bowel syndrome, eating disorder, allergies, insomnia, backaches, frequent cold and fatigue to diseases such as hypertension, asthma, diabetes, heart ailments and even Cancer. In fact, Sanjay Chugh, a leading Indian psychologist, says that 70 per cent to 90 per cent of adults visit primary care physicians for stress-related problems. This is scary enough, but where do we err?

Just about everybody men, women, children and even fetuses suffer from stress. Relationship demands, chronic health problems, pressure at workplaces, traffic snarls, meeting deadlines, growing-up tensions or a sudden bearish trend in the bourse can trigger stress conditions. People react to it in their own 'Nays. In some people, stress-induced adverse feelings and anxieties tend to persist and intensify. Learning to understand and manage stress can prevent the counter effects of stress.

Sources of Stress

Sources of stress might be evident in frustration, conflicts and pressures:

Frustration

Frustration results when our motives are thwarted, either by some obstacle that blocks or impedes our progress toward a desired goal, or by the absence of an appropriate goal. For example, overly-restrictive parents would be a source of frustration for the girl who wanted to go to a school party, while a lack of water would be a source of frustration to a man lost in the desert. Frustration may be minor, or they may be serious threats to our welfare; they may arise from outer or inner sources.

External Frustration

External frustration might be both physical and social, which can lead to frustration of our needs and efforts. Famines, droughts, storms, fires, earthquakes, injuries, accidents and the death of loved ones are major sources of thwarting in the physical environment. In addition, there are the more commonly experienced minor frustrating situations such as car trouble when we are in a hurry or rain when we wish to play tennis or golf.

Internal Frustration

On the other hand, internal frustration may be caused due to internal factors. Personal limitations in the form of physical handicaps, insufficient ability or lack of social charm, may all become sources of frustration in the fiercely competitive struggle for social recognition, success, martial partners, and status. Failures resulting from personal limitations and mistakes are likely to be serious sources of self-devaluation and frustration, particularly when such failures involve our key motives and purposes. Many internal frustrations arise out of psychological barriers in the form of reality and ethical controls. Biological conditions such as fatigue and disease are common and important sources of stress.

Conflict

Sometimes conflict play an important role in the causation of frustration. Often the frustration comes not from a single obstacle but from a conflict between two needs or valued goals, in which choosing either alternative means frustration with regard to the other. Complete sexual gratification may involve lowered self-esteem and social disapproval, or an early marriage may mean foregoing a college degree. Such incompatible action systems usually require a decision on the part of the individual and, as we shall see, may play an important part in the development of mental illness.

Conflicts with which all of us have to cope may be conveniently classified into approach-avoidant, double-approach, and double-avoidant conflicts.

Approach - avoidant conflict

In approach-avoidant conflicts there are strong tendencies both to approach and to avoid the same goal. A person may want to marry for sexual, social, and security reasons. While at the same time he fears the responsibilities and loss of personal freedom. He has tendencies both to approach and to avoid marriage. In a similar way his desires may conflict with his inner reality or ethical restraints or with fear of failure.

Double-approach conflict

Double-approach conflicts involve competition between two or more desirable goals. On a simple level the individual may have to decide between two motives or two makes of automobiles, or between steak and fish for dinner. In more complex cases he may be torn between duty and ambition, between loyalty to his mother and to his wife, between a legal and a medical career, or between present satisfactions and future ones.

Double-avoidant conflict

In double-avoidant conflicts the individual is completely hemmed in - he is caught 'between the Devil and the deep blue sea.' He may have to choose between unemployment and his job which he dislikcs, between marrying someone he does not love and the possibility that he will be unable to find anyone else. In wartime, he may have to choose between fighting, with the possibility of being killed, and social disapproval, with feelings of being a coward.

Conflicts are important sources of stress and frequently lead to such tension and inner turmoil that the individual's adjustive capacities are seriously impaired. In our society, adjustive difficulties are particularly common in the handling of conflicts centering around dependence vs. self-direction, contradictory values, and sexual desires vs. restraints.

Pressure

Pressure often makes individual's adjustment poor which leads to stress. Problems of adjustment may stem not only from frustrations and conflicts but also from pressures that complicate our strivings. Parents who have made sacrifices to send their son to college may exert a great deal of pressure on him for high achievement, and he may feel under considerable pressure not to let them down. Similarly a business executive may be under heavy and sustained pressure by virtue of the sheer number of important decisions he has to make each day. Such pressures force us to intensify our efforts and to speed up our activity - often to an uncomfortable degree. Even minor pressures can build up to a point where they involve severe stress. Pressures, like frustrations, may stem from inner or outer sources.

Inner pressure

Inner pressures typically involve our self-ideal and level of aspiration. Often we strive to live up to unrealistically high standards of ethical behaviour, courage and social responsibility - to fit the picture of ourselves as we think, we could and should be. Many of us drive ourselves mercilessly toward high levels of achievement. We are determined to get to the top, to be the best, to 'succeed'. In our highly competitive society, such aspirations can subject us to continuous and severe pressure and considerable discomfort.

Outer pressure

Many pressures arise from environmental demands which are called outer pressure. Parents may exert pressure on their children to get good grades; wives may exert pressure on their husbands to make more money; children may make severe demands on their parents' time and energy. Education, marriage, parenthood, occupation and civic responsibilities all exert pressures. Sometimes the sheer details of living subject put us to considerable pressure, and we feel confronted by a never ending stream of problems to be solved, decisions to be made, and deadlines to be met.

Stress Reaction : Physiological and Psychological

Selye describes antecedents of the stress concept in the Hippocratic view of disease not only as suffering but as toil : the fight of the body to restore itself. A recurring theme is a definite amount of 'adaptation energy' which gets 'used up' (Selye, 1950); or physiological and psychological integrative capacities which are taxed to the limit (Bosowitz et al; 1955).

The nature of pituitary–adrenal involvement has been much debated and the physiological (hormonal, metabolic, and so on) mechanisms involved in the stress reaction have been extensively investigated. (Goldstein & Ramay, 1957, Oken, 1967)

Attempts to extend Selye's idea of systematic stress to include psychological aspects, have met with many problems. Firstly, the nature of stressors is very different. Selye discussed such systematic stressor agents as heat, cold, infections, intoxicants, injury, shock and surgical trauma. The ranges of psychological stressors is so wide as to be virtually endless. Cofer & Apply argue that these are effective only when they threaten the life or integrity of the individual is exposed to them. They offer a definition of stress as 'the state of an organism when he perceives that his well-being (or integrity) is edangered and that he must elevate all of his energies to its protection.' (Cofer & Apply, 1964, P-453).

Secondly, the nature of the psychological reaction is not seen as general, well defined pattern. The results of research suggest that individual differences, styles, patterns of response and pre-potent tendencies lead to idiosyncratic response patterns. These may be related to inherited responsibility like sympathetic nervous systems (Eysenck, 1967) and possibly to various personality characteristics which determine stress thresholds and stress tolerance.

Central issues in psychological stress are the continuous processes (a) that lead the individual to differentiate between benign and damaging conditions, and (b) that determine the kind of coping behaviour which ensures. Recent analyses emphasize the role of cognitive appraisal (Lazarus, 1966). Once a stimulus has been appraised of threatening, various method of coping are adopted. Pribrams (1967) has suggested that cognitive re-evaluation may obviate the necessity for over behavioural adjustment : that is, an individual's appraisal of the situation can reduce the stress reactions.

When examined in a psychological context, the stress reaction, and feedback form the effects of these reactions. In such Circumstances it is difficult to retain. Selye's clear though perhaps over- simplified view of stress, and of late the meaning of the term has tended to widen again. For example it is often undifferentiated from anxiety, conflict, emotion, frustrations, and arousal (Q.V.).

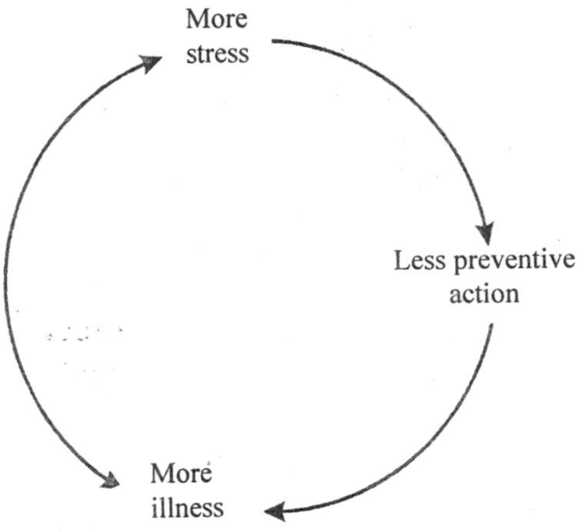

Fig. 3. The effects of stress, illness, and preventive action as seen in chain reaction : cited for research purpose.

It is of no doubt that some people are more prone to suffer from the effects of stress, but no one is immune to it. Only the threshold varies. Stress affects different parts of the body and can lead to various diseases. It has been observed that episodes of illness tend to cluster around periods when the individual perceived his life situation stressful. Alexander observed that when frustrations and conflicts are serious and of long duration and when the anxiety produced by them is not controlled in some way, the body remains in a constant state of mobilization. After a time this strain may result in certain physiological dysfunctions. Physiological disorders due to chronic and exaggerated emotional states are referred to as psychophysiologic reactions or psychosomatic disorders.

The repeated stress causes the heart to be overactive. The arteries become thicker, blood pressure increases and the heart has to work even harder to pump the blood throughout the body. It is suggested that lack of control over stress may be an important factor in producing hypertension.

Thus stress is known to give rise to a variety of non-specific biochemical, physiological and behavioural responses. There are enough evidences to support the actiological role of stress in various diseases in general and cardiovascular diseases in particular. Psychological stresses are also said to be associated with the causation as well as with the clinical course of isochronic heart disease. There are considerable evidences to suggest that stress plays definite role in the causation of hypertension, and that certain personality factors may be associated with the disease.

Stress Can Be Positive

The words 'positive' and 'stress' may not often go together. But, there are innumerable instances of people rising to the challenge of stress and as achieving unachievable, scientists stressing themselves out over a point to bring into light the most unthinkable secrets of the phenomenal world, and likewise a painter, a composer or a writer producing the best paintings, the most lilting tunes, the most appealing piece of writing by pushing themselves to the limit. Psychologists second the opinion that some 'stress' situations can actually boost our inner potential and can be creatively helpful. Sudha Chandran,an Indian, lost both of her legs in an accident. But, the physical and social inadequacies gave her more impetus to carry on with her dance performances with the help of prosthetic legs rather than deter her spirits.

Experts tell that stress, in moderate doses, are necessary in our life. Stress responses are one of our body's best defense systems against outer and inner dangers. In a risky situation (in case of accidents or a sudden attack on life et al), body releases stress hormones that instantly make us more alert and our senses become more focused. The body is also prepared to act with increased strength and speed in a pressure situation. It is supposed to keep us sharp and ready for action.

Research suggests that stress can actually increase our performance. Instead of wilting under stress, one can use it as an impetus to achieve success. Stress can stimulate one's faculties to delve deep into and discover one's true potential. Under stress the brain is emotionally and biochemically stimulated to sharpen its performance.

A working class mother in down town California, Erin Brokovich, accomplished an extraordinary feat in the 1990s when she took up a challenge against the giant industrial house Pacific Gas & Electric. The unit was polluting the drinking water of the area with chromium effluents. Once into it, BrockoVich had to work under tremendous stress taking on the bigwigs of the society. By her own account, she had to study as many as 120 research articles to find if chromium VI was carcinogenic. Going from door to door, Erin signed up over 600 plaintiffs, and with attorney Ed Masry went on to receive the largest court settlement, for the town people, ever paid in a direct action lawsuit in the U.S. history-$333 million. It is an example of an ordinary individual triumphing over insurmountable odds under pressure. If handled positively, stress can induce people to discover their inherent talents.

Stress is, perhaps, necessary to occasionally clear cobwebs from our thinking. If approached positively, stress can help us evolve as a person by letting go of unwanted thoughts and principle in our life. Very often, at various crossroads of life, stress may remind us of the transitory nature of our experiences, and may prove us to look for the true happiness of life.

College girls face a specific kind of stress. It could be problem at home, society, personal, physical or social like:

- high competition of jobs-feeling that there are no jobs out there
- Education choices-after college, paying for higher education
- stress of living at home, but yet feeling old enough to be on your own
- financial pressure-part time work is scarce and parents don't have as much money as they did twenty-twenty five years ago
- dysfunction families-girls from broken families, alcoholic, or abusive families
- blended families-girls may feel out of place.

Stress of college life is a significant factor for individual's proper growth. College students, in the transition period between late adolescence and early adulthood, have many special stresses with which they must contend. Exams, grades, sex, and pressure from parents create high levels of stress. More students drop out of college for emotional reasons than because of low grades.

The typical problems of college students involve guilt and confusion over the handling of sexual impulses, concern about the expression of hostile and aggressive feelings, and worry about personal inadequacy and lack of status. Many additional problems, more or less peculiar to the college student, contribute to the forces which interfere with personality adjustment.

For more than one hundred thousand college students who threaten suicide each year, about nine thousand actually attempt to kill themselves, and more than a thousand are successful in taking their lives. Excluding auto accidents, suicide is the leading cause of death among college students (NIMH, 1969).

A study at the University of California at Berkley found that college students who killed themselves were generally above average in scholastic attainment. Such students doubled their own adequacy, were dissatisfied with their grades, and were despondent over their general academic aptitude. They set unreasonably high standards for themselves and became depressed when they failed to meet these standard.

One student said, 'I felt I was different, I just plain didn't know how to get along with other people, as if there was something missing in me. I hated my parents, and I hated myself because of them. They convinced me that I was no good, that whatever I did, was nothing compared to what my two brothers did before me. I just couldn't please myself. My parents bounded me about my grades to the point where I couldn't study. They kept telling me 'You'll never make it'. By the end of the fall, I was so depressed. Failure was the worst thing in the world that could happen. I remember going home for Thanks giving vacation, and the leaves had fallen. It was wet and cold. My midterm exams had been dreadful. I was depressed worse than ever. Then it happened. Then came 30 sleeping pills, a bottle of aspirin and razor blade' (Sheperd, 1967).

Understanding Neurotic Behaviour

In the psychological literature the concept of neurosis has been elaborated in general as a form of 'mental disorder'. Neurosis may be considered as the outward and visible sign of an inward and invisible conflict between certain innate tendencies and moral religious percepts imposed upon mind. According to Scheier & Cattell (1961) 'Neuroticism is sometime defined as those personality characteristics, which actually he regards that true neurosis is largely dominated by unconscious.

It may be summarized that neurotics implies sensitivity, day-dreaming, shyness toward opposite sex, self-consciousness, emotionality, lack of realism, feeling of dependence, lack of initiative and enterprise, indecisive, inferiority feeling, lack of confidence and courage, unusual anxiety manifestation in physical tremor, depression, withdrawal, lack of concentration, nervousness, disturbed sleep (insomnia), suspicion, pessimism and restlessness.

The collective term 'neurosis' covers a wide range of different psychological symptoms and illnesses. Life entails growth, which progresses according to not only biological, but also psychological and social laws of development. The successful growth of a human being requires specific conditions for each phase of development. Impairment of this process of development can lead to illness and disability, which can, in turn, be significant for vocational rehabilitation. From the point of view of vocational integration, there are many parallels between young people with neuroses and those with psychoses.

The word neurotic is popular and widely used in day to day conversation. Most of the time people use it incorrectly and without any real knowledge of its meaning. A newspaper reporter described the murderer of an entire family as being 'neurotic' when in fact the killer showed all the sign of a far more serious mental disorder. The essential sequence in the development of the psychoneurotic disorders is typically : (a) faulty personality development – immaturity, distortions – resulting in specific weakness in personality structure, (b) evaluation of certain common life stress as terribly dangerous and threatening, (c) arousal of severe anxiety, (d) development of neurotic defensive patterns to cope with the threat and anxiety, and finally (e) vicious circles with lowered efficiency and a myriad of secondary symptoms such as chronic fatigue and dissatisfaction.

Origins of Neuroses

Neurotic disorders can have a variety of causes. A deprived or even damaging social background harms psychological and often also biological growth. Early deficiencies (ego weakness, lack of basic confidence or of social competence) have an effect on later phases of development, just as faults in the foundations of a house have an effect on all the floors above. 'Organic' development requires parents to 'let go' of their child so that he/she can move into a new phase of development. If the environment is over-protective, thus hindering this process of letting go, there will be no real need to take the next developmental steps and emotional growth may be stunted as a result.

Patterns of Neurotic Behaviour

According to this natural law of life, neurotic behaviour can be seen as an unsuccessful attempt to deal with these problems. The ability to cope with continually new challenges – and, at the same time, to dispel ever-present anxieties – requires courage, competence and confidence. If viability is underdeveloped, anxiety takes over and reduces the scope for action. Neurotic reactions do not solve any problems, but merely reduce this ever-present anxiety, with the result that the individual has less strength and attention left for solving the actual problems. In the long term, this unsucessful form of reaction devours more and more energy (progression), in the way that addiction to a drug means that increasingly higher doses are needed in order to achieve the desired effect. In some cases, the neurotic individual is resourceful and often amazingly creative in finding apparent ways of avoiding anxiety.

Starting points for neurotic behaviour are individual disposition, upbringing and behavioural patterns in one's social surroundings. The followings are some examples of general patterns of neurotic behaviour aimed at avoiding anxiety and therefore mature solutions:

- Resorting to behaviour which rekindles feelings of childhood security (regression);
- Retreating into an imaginary world where one's problems have been solved and where one already possesses all those abilities (heroism) necessary for overcoming anxiety-ridden reality (self-idealisation, feelings of omnipotence);
- Taking the route of medication and simply anaesthetising one's anxiety away (drugs, alcohol, work, smoking, TV);
- Letting unimportant details take over, or transforming the worrying aspects of a situation into manageable forms and dealing with them in a strictly regimented fashion (management) with which one feels safe and in control (evasive tactics, compulsive behaviour);
- Performing exaggerated rituals which give the impression of activity and divert one's energies away from the anxiety (compulsion);
- Attaching oneself to other people in search of earlier feelings of chilhood security (symbiosis, bonding);
- Analysing problems without being involved with them (rationalisation, cynisism);
- Evading problems, retreating into sickness and thus also gaining sympathy (secondary advantage of sickness);

- Redefining reality and dismissing any situations causing anxiety (denial, lying, looking the other way);
- Diverting internal tension outwards and expressing it by harming others, that is, by replacing anxiety with rage (aggression);
- Withdrawing and allowing one's own inner energies to dry up (depression);
- Turning aggression inwards or obliterating oneself (self-destruction, suicide).

Patterns of neurotic behaviour are to be found in every human being in one form or another and to varying degrees. They only cause problems when they are fixed to the extent that they become a syndrome. Here, the borderline between 'normality' and psychological illness is indistinct.

General symptoms

These so-called neurotic patterns of behaviour are often very successful in stemming the flow of anxiety, but do not lead to any mature, realistic resolution of a situation. In the medium-term, they can hamper the process of development in the phase of life reached; in the long-term, they can lead to stagnation. As one gets older, efforts employed to resolve matters are not only unsuccessful but become increasingly inappropriate requiring more and more energy. If the neurosis progresses in this way, it can turn into a serious psychological illness involving natural energy being misdirected, the loss of functional ability, zest for life, sexuality and contact with other people, one's own body and behaviour. The followings are the effects of neurotic development:

Psychopathy

Lack of the satisfaction and self-assurance, normally gained from successful participation in life, leads to a condition in which the individual permanently takes offence (narcisstic offence, a weak sense of ego). To compensate for this, the neurotic individual tries to find opportunities to bolster his/her ego with feelings of apparent strength. Disposition, negative influences in youth and a weak sense of ego can sow the seeds of future psychopathic substitute behaviour (perversions, substitute actions, compulsions, addictions).

Problems with relationships

Much so-called neurotic behaviour is really an one-sided, inappropriate attempt to deal with the problems in one's own life. People often cling to old solutions which no longer apply due to the process of natural development and the requirements of the stage of life reached. This increases with age, thus it is no longer possible to have equal relationships at work, in partnerships or within a circle of friends. The balance between closeness and distance is disturbed. On the one hand, there is a childlike yearning to attach oneself to others (symbiosis) and, on the other, excessive anxiety about losing one's own identity within a relationship. Where there is an inability to bond, there is generally a great danger of dependency developing as an immature form of relationship.

Restricted development

The more a neurotic individual evades anxiety, the more obsessive it becomes. This necessitates an increase in defence (a protective shield). Increasing attention must be paid to avoid imminent danger and the associated anxiety (avoidance). The neurosis takes up an ever increasing amount of energy during the course of the individual's life and gradually limits his/her scope for action. The apparent solution to problems becomes a predominant pattern. A predisposition to solve problems more by management and ritual (as described above) can become a compulsive feature of the personality. Escaping into illness can lead to serious psychosomatic disorders. A tendency to reject life when offended can set into depression. Neurotic actions turn into neurotic characteristics.

Systematic effects

This obstacle in the growth process stunts productivity, reduces the scope for action and is a strain on relationships. Family, children and colleagues, and even one's own body, are drawn into this neurotic way of life. Children can assume the symptoms of the neurotic behaviour they are confronted with and this sows the seeds of a new developmental disorder.

Specific syndromes

Neuroses can consolidate into any of large number psychological illnesses, which can also overlap each other. The following symptoms are most important in terms of career choice among college girls.

Several neurotic symptom patterns have been delineated here for consideration :

Anxiety reaction

This is the most common of the various psychoneurotic reaction patterns, constituting about 30 to 40 per cent of all neurotic disorders. This reaction differs from other neurotic reactions in that the anxiety is experienced directly — hence the anxiety is said to be 'free floating.' In anxiety reactions there is a relatively constant state of tension, restlessness, and diffused uneasiness. The individual exhibits generalized irritability, has difficulty in concentrating, and suffers from insomnia. Usually he has difficulty in making decisions and dreads the possibility that he may make a mistake. There may be mild nausea, loss of appetite, and some loss of weight. He may have heart palpitations for no apparent reason, and may have cardiovascular changes such as elevated blood pressure and an increased pulse rate (Gunn, 1962). In essence, the individual suffers from a chronic state of alarm and mobilization.

Neurotic worries and fears are capable of causing a number of disturbances in many individuals. A neurosis of this type produces a chronic state of tension. In this group we find those persons who are victimized by all sorts of anxiety fears like; fears of elevator, crowds, germs, sex insanity, death and many others. Their feeling of insecurity keeps them on edge. They never relax. They are in a constant state of nervous exhaustion. Whatever the particular neurosis may be, the psychology of its development is practically the same. Fear-thinking neurotics are victims of unconscious motivations. In any event, neurosis is curable.

Neurosis is the general term for impairment of emotional growth and the resulting problems. Anxiety plays a decisive role in neurotic disorders. From a positive point of view, anxiety is an important warning sign of risks and dangers. From a negative point of view, excessive anxiety can block natural development. The two basic forms of anxiety suffered by human beings are :

- separation anxiety, when the safe, familiar or trusted must be left, and
- situation or attachment anxiety, when facing new, strange or unfamiliar situations.

Anxiety can exist as a phobia of individual objects or situations. It can, however, also be a prevailing mood influencing one's life. In normal development, the play instinct, curiosity and zest for life are natural opposing forces which help to overcome anxiety and stimulate the developmental process. For this, one needs confidence in oneself and in one's parents, friends and colleagues.

Asthenic reaction (Neurasthenia)

An asthenic reaction is a characteric assortment of vague aches and pains. The person having difficulty in concentrating, is easily distracted, and lacks the vigour required to carry activities for successful completion. Even minor tasks seem to require Herculean effort. He sleeps poorly and feels 'just rotten' when he drags himself out of bed in the morning. He is completely upset by minor emotional setbacks, such as some criticism of his behaviour, and his fatigue and restlessness return. In addition to chronic fatigue, the neurasthenic usually has a variety of other somatic complaints like headaches or stuffiness of the head, indigestion, pain in the small of the back, dizzy spells, hypersensitivity to minor irritations, and feeling of weakness. Neuro-asthenia fatigue is the predominating symptom, although the neurasthenic may also complain of vague aches and pain.

Conversion reaction (Hysteria)

Conversion reactions is a neurotic defense in which symptoms of some physical illness appear without any underlying organic pathology. It is one of the most intriguing and baffling of all the psychopathological syndromes. Conversion reactions may simulate a wide range of organic illness, and the specific symptoms that may occur are legion. In this reaction patent avoids or solves some problems of getting sick. The symptoms protect him from facing the traumatic situation and at the same time bringing him secondary gains in extra sympathy and attention as well as some control over the people around him.

Emotional instability is the most characteristic symptom. The mental conflicts express themselves through symptoms that affect various parts of the body. For example, a wife who is unhappily married may complain to her husband about her 'backaches' Psychiatrists use the term 'conversion symptoms' because it actually describes what happens when the unhappiness or mental conflict is converted into an actual physical symptom.

This personality (mostly women) is self-centered with frequent emotional outbursts and histrionic display. This is the result of over-protection and spoiled childhood. Their dramatic behaviour is to attract attention or get their way. When faced with frustration, they throw temper tantrum or put on a violent scene. Many of those women are provocative and exhibitionistic with men. Their purpose is to control or have a victory over them rather than deeper relationship.

Dissociative reaction

Dissociative reactions, often classified as one type of hysteria, include amnesia, fugul, multiple personality, and somnambulism. In each case, the patient successfully blocks off part of his life from conscious recognition. In psychogenic amnesia, one's typically finds an egocentric, immature, highly suggestable personality faced with an acutely unpleasant situation from which he sees no escape. He tries to avoid some unpleasant situation by getting sick. He does it by forgetting (repressing or suppressing) certain traumatic events or stress. Multiple personality is a dissociative reaction to stress in which the patient manifests two or more complete systems of personality. Each system has distinct, well-developed emotional and thought processes and represents unique and relatively stable personality. Somnambulism is another neurotic dissociative reaction in which the ideas are blocked off from consciousness which are strong enough to determine the patient's behaviour, though only during sleep. The episodes may occur nightly or only irregularly. They are most common in adolescence, but may occur in childhood or during adult life. Gorgenes (1941) reported that 5 per cent of a group of 1808 college freshmen admitted walking in their sleep. Sleepwalking is much more common among males than among females.

Phobic reaction

A phobic reaction is a persistent fear of some object or situation which presents no actual damage to the patient or in which is magnified in all proportion to its actual seriousness. Patients usually admit that they have no real cause to be afraid of the object or situation but say that they cannot help themselves. Phobias are attempts to cope with internal or external damages by preventing their occurrence or carefully avoiding them. Thus phobias are considered simple defensive reactions.

'Organic' development of a human being increases the ability to deal with threatening situations. Disturbed development leads to reduced competence and confidence so that increasingly smaller incidents trigger greater anxiety attacks, which are usually accompanied by physical symptoms. A phobia is a fear linked with specific objects or situations and is a trigger of anxiety. In a neurotic cycle of behaviour, more and more energy is expended in detecting threatening situations, which cause anxiety, and in evading them (avoidance). In addition, there is the tendency for anxiety to spread (generalization) to a multitude of stimuli. Here, too, the rule applies that succumbing to a phobia only results in its becoming stronger. Phobias can affect virtually all activities and all areas of life (e.g. people, situations, rooms, places, heights, animals, failure, incompetence, illness).

Obsessive - Compulsive reaction

In obsessive – compulsive reactions, as with phobias, the person recognizes the irrationality of his behaviour, but seems compelled to think about something that he wishes not to think about or to carry out actions that he does not want to carry out. Obsessive thoughts may centre around a wide variety of topics, from concern over bodily functions to suicide or to the solutions of some scientific problem. Particularly common are obsessive fears of uncontrollable impulses. In compulsive reactions the person feels compelled to perform some act which, even during the process, seems absurd and strange to him. Neurotic obsessive - compulsive reaction, by contrast, are considered faulty adjustive techniques because they represent exaggerated defenses in the face of stress which are not unduly upsetting of the normal person and because they make for rigidly of behaviour and restriction of the individual's personality.

It is a personality trait disturbance characterized by an exaggerated sense of responsibility and an excessive need for perfection. Compulsive personality has difficulty of making up his mind, totally incapable of relaxing. A compulsive worker insists on clean desk; a housewife who spends her life on dusting and picking up. They create unnecessary work for self and others. They had often over-critical parents and therefore have repressed anger and hostility.

These individuals show anxiety neurosis and obsessive-compulsive reaction. They are morally rigid, unable to give expression to their love and hate feelings, unstable concepts of themselves, unsure of their goals, unsatisfactory and distorted sex lives, feelings of insecurity, guilt, self-doubt and make excessive use of defence reactions.

The obsessive personality is characterized by perfectionism, excessive orderliness, indecisiveness and constant worry over trifles. They must have their desk or room arranged in a certain order, eat at certain times and pay a lot of attention to cleanliness. Irritate others by imposing rigid standards; keep others waiting when they have to make up their minds. Obsessive personality, if expressed to continuing stress, they develop neurosis.

Compulsions (anancasma) is the situations causing anxiety, certain evasive actions and thoughts can help to reduce nervous tension. They have a similar effect to drugs. Almost all types of actions and thoughts can be used in this way. These patterns of behaviour can become more and more ingrained (ritualisation) until serious compulsive illness develops which often proves to be very resistant to therapy. Fundamental to such development are individual disposition and upbringing. As with addiction, a feature of this condition is that anxiety increases at the same rate as giving way to the compulsive urges. Once a serious compulsive illness has developed, it is very difficult to break it. It is important to recognise the early signs and to take therapeutic counter measures. The advanced stages of compulsive neuroses place a great strain on those around the sufferer and impose increasing limits on personal freedom and development.

Neurotic depressive reaction

All of us have the blues sometimes and many becomes greatly depressed at the death of a loved one, a disappointment in love, an accident, some occupational setback, or feelings of guilt concerning failure or unethical desires or behaviour. In neurotic depressive reactions, the individual reacts to some distressing stress situations with more than the usual amount of sadness and dejections and often fails to return to normal after a reasonable period of time. Although such reactions may last for weeks or even months, they do eventually clear up. In some cases a mildly depressed mood remains after more severe symptoms have abated. The neurotic depressive's symptoms make the performance of his everyday tasks difficult but usually not impossible. His major difficulty seems to lie in his inability to concentrate and in lowered levels of activity and initiative. However, in very severe reactive depressions the patient may be unable to work and may sit alone hopelessly staring into space, able to see only the dark side of life.

An individual's natural development can be greatly disturbed by external influences (e.g. maltreatment, long periods of imprisonment, loss of job or of a beloved partner, lack of love). These shattering experiences can result in an individual withdrawing from life. Regression to patterns of childlike behaviour is a natural way of trying to reduce feelings of upset and sorrow. However, if sorrow becomes so overwhelming that it prevents further development, it is referred to as depression (to be differentiated from depressive reaction). It leads to considerably limited scope for development and action. The longer a case of depression lasts, and the more it is labeled as such by outsiders, the more it becomes part of the individual's character (depressive character). Retreat into an ever-shrinking private world follows. The vibrant aspects of life gradually disappear. Depression always involves loneliness. Uppermost are problems of mood (exhaustion, indifference, hopelessness) and drive (inhibition, lack of initiative, paralysis, restriction). There is often compulsion (worrying, the mind going round in circles) and obsessive thought (feelings of guilt, impoverishment, failure, worthlessness). The neurosis seriously affects the way in which one relates not only to other people but also to one's own body (appetite, sleep, potency, menstrual cycle). With depressive illnesses, the risk of suicide is particularly high. Today, therapy relies heavily on medication, which makes it possible to lighten the mood of the individual and to increase his/her drive. Primarily, however, psychotherapy is needed to treat the neurotic disposition or condition in order to penetrate the cycle of depression. The alternative is for the individual to learn how to deal with upsets and unavoidable separations. If there is a history of suicide attempts, extensive help will be required and those around the individual affected, are often incapable of providing this.

Neurotics are chronic worries. Individuals who are excessively sensitive, over-aggressive, extremely shy, or easily depressed and who indulge in negative thinking, are inclined to be tense and nervous with or without provocation. They do not react well to personal frustrations. They are inclined to be dreamers rather than doers. As Claude Bristol in 'The Magic of Believing', puts it, they have a wishbone but no backbone.

However, if one probes into their inner personality, one will find that basically they are nice people. The neurotic, who is self-centered and self-conscious, needs to be made un-self-conscious. Nothing so much militates against his recovery, as humiliating him by making him feel responsible for his illness.

Apart from above said specific syndromes of neurotic behaviour there are some others as follows :

Suicide

Developments can take people to the stage where they can see no way out other than to take their own life. Characteristic of this condition is an increasingly narrow range of perception, thought and ability to act (pre-suicidal syndrome). There is usually a history of long-term unsolved problems and increasing isolation. Attention is focused less on solving problems than on controlling anxieties. Medication and alcohol usually play a part in this process. The failure to find solutions and the sense of isolation together result in a feeling of being trapped for which suicide appears to be the only answer. This is intensified if there is a personal or family history of suicide or suicide attempts, since suicide is subconsciously recognised as a way out. Examples of further factors contributing to a risk of suicide are endogenous depression, schizophrenia, addiction, serious illness, isolation, a lack of purpose in life and unemployment.

Psycho-somatic disorders

Psychosomatic disorders are those in which emotional or psychic disturbances are responsible for organic or physical disorders. This includes essential hypertension, bronchial asthma, ulcerative colitis, migraine headaches, arthritis, peptic and duodenal ulcer. Encephalitis, tuberculosis, diabetes mellitus, sexual dysfunction, diarrhoea, obesity, skin diseases, fevers, chills, cough, itching ears, chest pain, eye trouble, constipation, sore throat, abdominal cramps, sterility and Parkinson's disease are example of somatopsychic disorders.

At the base of these psychosomatic and somato-psychic disorders, lies emotional disturbance, particularly emotional conflict. Emotional disturbance affects the weakened organ. It is also the attitude of the patient towards life situation disturbing him. These are also the results of personality development and communication difficulties in interpersonal situations. The modern interpretation is that psycho-somatic or somato-psychic disorders are the results of inability to cope with stress situation.

Psychosomatic or somatopsychic disorders are affected by organs under the control of the autonomic nervous system where as neurosis and hysteric disorders are responsive to those regions of the body that respond to the central nervous system.

As body (soma) and soul (psyche) form one basic unit, it is understandable that disorders in one area will also affect the other. Serious physical illness has psychological consequences, and psychological disorders always have an effect on the body. This interaction can vary greatly depending on disposition (organic disposition) and upbringing (learning by imitation). The autonomic nervous system is the link between body and soul. Psychosomatic illness therefore appears mainly in systems that are influenced by the autonomic nervous system or by hormones. This is the case with, for example, colitis ulcerosa (inflammation of the lining of the large intestine), ulcers, asthma, problems with digestion, the heart or circulation (internal diseases), eczema (skin diseases), migraine, hypertonia (high blood pressure) and sleeping disorders. With psychosomatic disorders, the organic and psychological aspects can be of varying importance. Organic conditions (e.g. allergies) can be made worse by psychological causes. Therefore, over-hasty diagnosis of a condition as being psychogenic should be avoided, since this could mean that organic causes are overlooked. Treatment of these disorders should always involve body and soul simultaneously.

Hypochondriasis

It is often heard someone referred to as a 'hypochondriac'. This means that there is always something ailing him, usually something imagined. He is over concerned about his health and enjoys talking about his many ailments. Once asked a woman patient to tell what she complained of? When she finished the recital, it is a list of 57 different symptoms. These people become 'professional' patients going from one doctor to another doctor for relief.

Schizoid personality

The characteristics of this personality are shyness, introversion, and a tendency to avoid social contact and close relationships. This type of person is usually aloof, detached, suffer from feelings of loneliness and inadequacy to express anger or endure competition and frequently retreat to inner world of fantasies and day dreams. They are cold, moody, ill-tempered and mistrustful; may enjoy poetry, writing and painting.

Eating disorders

Bulimia (addiction to eating or slimming), anorexia nervosa (potentially fatal addiction to slimming), adipositas (obesity). Eating disorders are usually caused by identity problems during puberty and particularly affect young girls (about 90 % of cases). This stage of life entails great physical and social adjustment. The body is reshaped and takes on new functions leading to a new identity as a woman. Childhood developmental problems and cultural and fashion trends (slimming cult, feminist movement) can all have considerable influence on the natural process of development during puberty.

Dependency, addiction

In the widest sense, 'drugs' are a rapid way of experiencing pleasant sensations without the long and often painful growing process. Drugs are a way of apparently overcoming the low points in life and of avoiding laborious detours. Resorting to 'drugs' (alcohol, cigarettes, drugs, sport, holidays – basically anything can become addictive) is always a form of regression into the feelings of security experienced at an early age. Childish phantasy worlds are maintained, and adult, mature ways of solving problems (taking responsibility) are avoided. However, the price to pay for this is the loss of freedom and self-respect. Different drugs take a different amount of time to cause physical addiction, differ in their tendency to require increasing doses to reach the desired effect, and lead to different withdrawal symptoms, some of which can be extremely painful. In the medium term, they destroy the individual and his/her professional and social life. Today's society, with its emphasis on consumerism and thrills, provides all the basic conditions for the neurotic path of addiction and dependency. This holds dangers for the young individual who has not yet reached a state of emotional equilibrium. The number of people falling victim to addictions are thus increasing greatly. Without first changing the basic social situation, purely repressive measures cannot solve the problem. Prevention, rehabilitation and therapy are based on an attempt to build up the individual's ego, stability and competence and hence to enable him/her to take responsibility for meeting the challenges of life, to grow with this and thereby experience genuine fulfilment.

Neurosis as disability

Neurotic disorders are often regarded as merely temporary problems and therefore tend to be classed as 'mild disabilities'. General laws of development, however, clearly show that there is often a very deep-seated disorder of the whole predisposition to life which only fully develops in later years. In early years, it is often possible to compensate for neurotic illness, but as one gets older, natural energy is often insufficient to maintain the necessary level of defence. In addition, at a young age, the healthy aspects of the character are not yet overwhelmed by neuroses. It is possible to differentiate between two types of neurosis:

- **Manifest neurotic symptoms**: Symptoms often cause serious problems for the individual and those around him or her. The degree of suffering, the noticeable symptoms and the progression of the illness are such that diagnosis is simple.
- **Concealed neurotic disorders**: The neurosis is part of a generally disturbed predisposition and not very noticeable. Symptoms are mostly compensated for and the individual is able to adapt sufficiently to social situations. However, the individual's personal history (periods of hospitalisation, psychotherapy, the need for parental counselling) provides an indirect indication of the situation. If no help is given, severe disability is a real danger. If therapy begins early and the personality has not yet become distorted, the outlook is favourable. In such cases, people such as careers advisers, teachers, doctors and psychologists have a great responsibility in the early recognition of imminent disabilities.

Career choice and Neurotic Behaviour

Social environment

Severe neurotic disorders involving very limited personal development and obvious neurotic symptoms can be very debilitating. A clear picture of the patient's history is needed in order to alter the development of the neurosis during puberty.

This involves examining the problems of the disabled young person and the social environment as well as looking at the history of his or her development. The dynamics of the family is a decisive factor in planning necessary measures. If the young person, seeking careers advice, is showing the symptoms of pathogenic family dynamics, a major aspect of therapy can entail removing him or her from the family environment (vocational rehabilitation with accommodation in a residential school). Making such an assessment can often be difficult and requires additional information from third parties (teachers, family doctor, relations).

Assessment of the disability

It is particularly difficult to make a diagnosis in the case of concealed neuroses where the young person's behaviour does not seem particularly unusual and it is necessary to ascertain whether severe disability is likely, if no therapy is undertaken. In these cases, it is often necessary to seek further advice (for example psychological, educational, medical) and the Careers Advice Service will usually involve the medical and Psychological Services of the Office of Employment (Arbeitsamt). Young people with neurotic symptoms usually have to participate in pre-vocational training programmes. When making a career choice, it is essential to bear in mind the fact that the chosen career should not present circumstances which will have a negative effect on the individual's neurotic make-up (disposition, character). This means that the occupation must correspond to personal interests and abilities (suitability), but it should not contribute to the further development of neuroses. A 'therapeutic' middle way must be found which is based on inclinations and which provides the scope for positive development. This applies particularly to compulsive disorders, problems of addiction and dependency, disorders of sexual identity and problems with relationships.

Vocational Integration and Neurotic Behaviour Principles of Rehabilitation

In terms of vocational integration, there are many parallels between young people with neuroses and those with psychoses. For this reason, only a basic outline of vocational rehabilitation is given here. As shown above, neuroses are developmental disorders. Thus, the fundamental principal of rehabilitation is to correct developmental faults, to make up for any developmental deficiencies, and to dispense with immature methods of handling problems by building up confidence. Unlike psychotherapy, the principal behind rehabilitation is to enable the individual to develop a sense of competence and worth by means of his/her own performance within a vocational training programme. In connection with the very varied aspects of social learning, this process is a way of correcting forms of neurotic development during adolescence by allowing the young person to mature. It is important that the young person can work from a stable and trusting relationship basis in order to confront new challenges. Since, with neuroses, the whole pattern of relationships (family, social environment) is often part of the neurotic system of dynamics, parental participation in rehabilitative measures is usually essential (secondary prevention). It is very important to make future plans for the individual's life and work after rehabilitation at an early stage in order to prevent the stability.

Broader Scope for Action

It should be remembered that neurotic behaviour represents an attempt to overcome excessive anxiety. This fundamentally neurotic method of mishandling a situation by avoiding it, rather than approaching it with maturity, is not unusual. It only becomes truly neurotic when it takes over the individual's behavioural pattern and increasingly limits his/her scope for action. Therefore, therapy cannot merely treat the neurotic symptoms from which the individual concerned and those around him or her begin to suffer, it must also correct the distorted emotional development. Above all, the individual's personal scope for action must be extended. The individual must resolve the neurosis by him or herself. Therapy can only assist in building up a sense of security and confidence so that anxieties can be more easily tolerated. Therapy is a learning process, which involves the maturing of emotions, and characteristics, which had previously remained underdeveloped. If it is too late to cure elementary faults, tactics must be devised to help compensating anxieties and to set the process of personal development into motion in order to create new freedoms. It should be recognized that the later in life, one tries to catch up on learning, the more difficult it becomes. Certain learning experiences require an appropriate learning environment. In adulthood, it is therefore difficult to reproduce childhood learning experiences in order to provide conditions for the necessary learning process. The sooner therapy begins, the more successful the process is likely to be. Thus, diagnosis is very important. Early therapy can prevent human suffering and also avoid the considerable costs of failed emotional development. For help to be effective, it is often necessary to remove the individual from surroundings which are the contributory factor to the illness.

Neurotics are not always failures

With insight and proper cooperation, the neurotic need not go through life handicapped. Once he understands the psychology of his neurotic personality, he can convert his neurosis into a blessing in disguise. One does not have to be glad that he is neurotic, neither does he has to be sad. Many famous figures in history who rose above the herd, were neurotic scientists, musician, artists, writers etc. They were neurotic in the sense that they were temperamental and sensitive. They lost control of their emotions. There are so many people who are neurotic. Many of them are very much talented and capable of making worthwhile contributions to life.

A study reported by Eysenck (1961) measured a group of normal subjects and six groups of neurotics on a battery of objective tests. Statistical analysis of the scores yielded two major factors, introversion - extroversion and neuroticism. As the group shows, the groups were well differentiated along with these dimensions. Eysenck's interpretation of these results is described in the text.

Summary Chart of Psychoneurotic Disorders

REACTION	*MAJOR SYMPTOMS*	*BASIC DYNAMICS*
ANXIETY	'Free floating' anxiety, usually punctuated by acute attacks	Mameling of internal or external threats by simple repression Anxiety not yet 'bound' or controlled by ego defenses
ASTHENIC	Feelings of weakness, fatigue, lack of enthusiasm; somatic complaints	Protection of self from anxiety aroused by unsatisfactory life situation in which individual feels trapped. Utter discouragement feels too tired and sick to continue fight
CONVERSION	Stimulation of actual organic illness – may involve varied sensory, motor, or somatic illness symptoms	Getting sick to escape from anxiety-arousing stress situation
DISSOCIATIVE	Amnesia, fugul, multiple personality, somnambulism	Escape from axiety-arousing conflicts by isolating or dissociating opposite

REACTION	*MAJOR SYMPTOMS*	*BASIC DYNAMICS*
		poles of the conflict; in fugul reaction, for example, the conflict between fighting and withdrawal is solved by between amnesic and running away.
PHOBIC	Irrational fears which individual realizes are irrational but which leads to anxiety, if not heeded	Persistent conditioned fear or defusive reaction to protect self from anxiety arousing stress by displacing anxiety from the actual danger to some symbolically related aspect of it which they protect the patient from facing the stress situation itself
OBSESSIVE-COMPULSIVE	Persistent thoughts or impulsive which the individual realize are irrational but which he cannot avoid	Defensive reactions, which protect the individual against internal ad external threats by substitutive activities, reaction formation, isolation of anxiety - arousing desires from their affective base, counteracting of fears by compulsive rituals and by an obsessive 'ordering' of the situation so that everything is under control and nothing can go wrong
NEUROTIC DEPRESSIVE	Feelings of dejection, discouragement, self - depreciation	Extreme discouragement resulting from environmental setbacks with part of the anxiety aroused by these setbacks allayed by intropumitiveness (self punishment)

Eysenck (1960, 1963) has emphasized the role of ease of conditioning in neurotic disorders. Because of greater autonomic reactivity, introverts presumably form quick and strong conditioned reactions and hence are prone to 'surplus conditioned reactions, involving fears and anxieties, which leave them vulnerable to diverse environmental stresses. On the other hand, extroverts presumably are deficient in the capacity to form conditioned reactions, fail to acquire many needed adaptive responses, and are deficient in socializations. They are weak in conscience development and are unwilling to take responsibility. On the basis of their studies Eysenck and Claridge (1962) concluded that anxiety reactions, phobic reactions, obsessive - compulsive reactions, and reactive depressions are introverted neuroses, while hysteria is an extroverted neurosis.

EYSENCK'S TWO - DIMENSIONAL FRAMEWORK

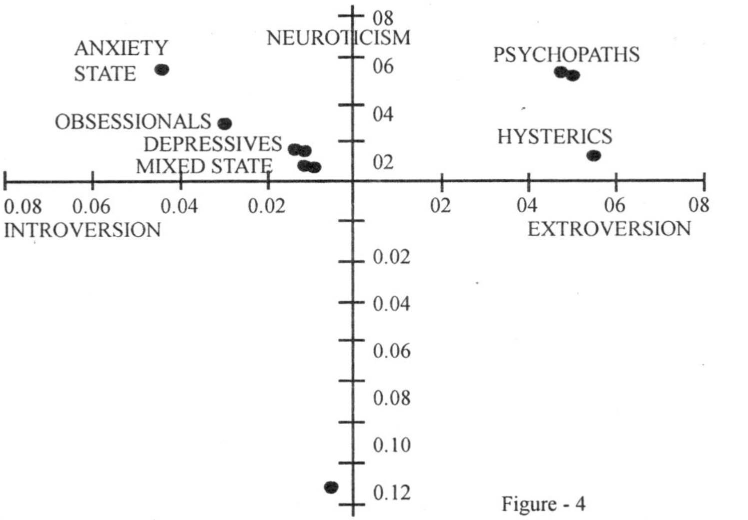

Figure - 4

Source : Coleman, James C (1970); Abnormal Psychology & Modern Life, Taraporevala Sons and Co. Bombay, (1970) : Cited for research purpose.

The neurosis is one of the most common forms of maladaptive behaviour. However, since the neurotic remains in contact with reality and is not a threat to the physical well-being of other people, confinement in a hospital or an institution is not required.

The scientific view of neurosis is that it is a pattern of maladaptive behaviour in which a person responds to life stress with persistent anxiety or other behaviour representing attempts to control the anxiety. The neurotic ordinarily recognizes the undesirable and sometimes disabling nature of his or her symptoms. There is no break with reality, and neurotic people usually do not need to be hospitalized.

While there is rather general agreement that neurotic behaviour is related to anxiety and the struggle to control it, there is considerable difference of opinion as to how neurosis develops and is maintained. As in the case of many other forms of maladaptive behaviour, it is unlikely that there is a simple or single explanation. Biological, psychological, and socio-cultural influences combine in varying degrees to determine whether or not a person becomes neurotic and what from a neurosis may take.

It would therefore be evident that stress and neurotic behaviour are important factors for proper adjustment in life. College life is a period in which an individual gets real understanding of society and individual's role into it. This is a life's formation period. It was, therefore, considered necessary to study the stress pattern and neurotic behaviour of college girls with a view to having a scientific understanding of the problem and providing solutions to adjustment level, if any. The present research was undertaken to fulfil the same academic and professional need.

2

Review of Literature

The literature concerning stress would be reviewed with a view to finding out the relationship between stress and certain psycho-social variables. While reviewing the literature, an effort would be made to see the nature of stress and the relationship of stress to drug abuse, smoking, performance, suicidal thoughts, post-traumatic stress, mental health, life events and social support, etc. The details of the review would be presented in the following paragraphs.

Stress : Nature

Almost all stress researchers experience some confusion and despair about the field. Indeed their is some doubt that the concept of stress is worth preserving. Pearline *et al* (1981) suggested that it is not the core meaning of the concept that is confusing, for there is general agreement that stress refers to a response of the organism to a noxious or threatening condition. The doubt and disagreement arise with regard to where and how to identify this response. Is stress, for example, to be recognized by the functioning of an organ or a system of organs, by bio-chemical or physiological alternations, by changes in emotional stress, or by the presence of disease entities? Is it manifested in short - run reactions of the organisms or in long-run dysfunction? Are people aware of the stress they harbour to the extent that they can report it, or must its presence be determined by independent assays ? Is stress a global, encompassing state, or is it confined to situations in which it is aroused ? The real problem in understanding stress is not that there are no answers to these questions, but that the answer to each of them is yes. That is, manifestations of stress are found at every level below consciousness. Finally, stress responses can be highly contained and situationally bounded, but they also can develop into a prevailing state that persists through time and extends through space.

It is in the very nature of stress that it can be of so many things, and one should not try to reduce the multidimensionality of this phenomenon by arbitrarily declaring that stress is only one thing or another. It is much more productive, the diffuse character of the stress phenomenon and to bend efforts to understanding how its multiple manifestations are interconnected. But it is not likely that this shift will occur quickly, for research into the various ways in which stress can be manifested, is closely organized around disciplines, and disciplinary lines are not easily breached. The social scientist is not likely to study the production of steroids, and the endocrinologist is equally unlikely to study the production of depression. Firmly and actively engaged in his chosen research, each investigator is convinced that the manifestations of stress that he is examining represent 'real' stress.

The concept of stress is varied despite its problems and shortcomings. It is not unusual in science for the same concept to acquire diverse meaning and to recruit the interest of many disciplines, the confusion that inevitably results is forgivable and should not inhibit continued work at multiple levels.

There were many studies available in the psychological literature in which efforts had been made to find out the impact of drug abuse and smoking on stress. Rohsenow *et al,* (1985), for example, reported a study entitled 'stress management training' as a prevention programme for heavy social drinkers and found that cognition affects drinking and individual differences. Treated and controlled subjects rated the frequency and intensity of their anxiety, anger, depression and recorded their alcohol consumption on a daily basis over a six month period. The men in the stress management training group showed a significant decrease in daily drinking rates at post treatment and at the 2½ month follow up, but drinking returned to baseline level by 5½ month for the group as a whole. However, significant improvement variance in daily moods and in drinking rates over all post-treatment periods was accounted for by individual differences variables in the trained subjects but not in the controlled group. This study suggested that these cognitive, personality and social support variables are associated with response to stress management training.

MacDougall *et al*, (1988) investigated the independent and joint effects of cigarette smoking and caffeine consumption on blood pressure and heart rate reactions to stress in male and female college students. Following an initial physiological baseline, participants received one of four experimental treatments (paced smoking, caffeine, smoking plus caffeine, or neither) and had blood pressure and heart rate measured before, during, and after two stressful tasks. The results revealed that, compared with the controled condition, caffeine ingestion enhanced the magnitude of stress induced systolic blood pressure and heart rate reactions. Smoking, combined additively with stress, and the joint effect of smoking and caffeine was no greater than either, taken alone. Males and females were generally similar in their blood pressure and heart rate responses to smoking, caffeine and stress.

Minugh and Harlow (1994) reported a study in which substance use factors were examined and cross validated in a cluster analytic approach in two independent samples of college students (N = 291 and N = 602). They reported frequency, intensity and amount of substance use were examined for beer, hard liquor, marijuana, amphetamines, barbiturates, psychedelics, cocaine, and heroin. Variables were reduced using principal component analysis to form four substance use composites. Composite scores were entered into four distinct clusters of substance use groups. External validity was obtained by showing that these four groups differed on a set of relevant variables. The four groups served as levels of the independent variable, substance use type in four MANOVAS examining group differences on peer and family influence, psycho-social functioning habit acquisition, and self-efficiency. Findings indicated that as frequency and intensity of substance use increased and individuals reported more problems in living, although a causal direction can not be established.

More recent researches have focussed upon life events, coping ability and stress. Nezu (1986), for example, reported a study entitled 'effects of stress from current problem comparison to major life events.' The present investigation evaluated the stressful effects of self defined problematic situations on consequent depressive and anxiety symptomatology. It was hypothesized that the frequency of problems would be a meaningful predictor of distress apart from the stress associated with major life changes. A prospective design was used to evaluate this predictive relationship. Further, prior levels of distress served as relevant covariates to control for premorbid status. Results from 129 college students were found to be supportive of the major hypothesis.

Hovonitz (1986) reported a study entitled 'life event stress and coping style as contributors to psychopathology'. This study evaluated the simultaneous contribution of life event stress and coping style as well as the independent contribution of each, to psychopathology. In the study 76 male and 74 female college students served as primary subjects, while an additional 57 male and 60 female college students served as a cross validation sample. Each subject completed the Life Experiences Survey, the Coping Strategies Inventory, and the MMPI. Sex differences were found in the type of coping style related to psychopathology, the relative contribution of coping style and negative life stress to psychopathology and the percentage of variance accounted for in psychopathology.

Jung and Khalsa (1989) reported a study in which Black and White American college students were compared to determine how daily hassles, coping strategies, and social support related to depression. Although the mean intensity of hassles did not differ, Black students reported a higher frequency of hassles. Cumulative severity of hassles, defined in terms of both intensity and frequency was therefore higher for Black students. White students perceived more support from friends than from family, but the opposite held for Black students. Mean scores on type of coping (active problem solving, seeking social support, or avoidance) were similar, as were the reported levels of depression. Hierarchical multiple regression showed that the severity of hassles was directly related to depression for both groups. Race did not interact with any index of social support, except perceived family support, which was related to lower depression among Black students. There was no support for the nation that social support serves as a buffer against depression.

Epstein and Katz (1992) in a study entitled 'coping ability, stress, productive load and symptoms' demonstrated with 450 college students (a) the importance of a distinction between self-produced and externally produced stressors, (b) the usefulness of a construct of productive load, and (c) stronger relation of the constructive Thinking Inventory that of the Hardiness Questionnaire, with productive load and with mental and physical symptoms. Because a major path, through which coping ability influences symptoms, is negative emotions, the widely recommended practice of partialing. Self-reported negative effect out of relations among coping, stress, and symptoms is often inappropriate. However, as total daily stressors (e.g., hassles) consist largely of self produced stressors, it is highly confounded with coping ability and it is therefore important to partial coping ability, out of relations between total stressors and other variables.

Spurrell *et al* (1994) reported a study entitled, 'post traumatic stress disorder and coping after a natural disorder'. They examined the role of coping in the onset of post traumatic stress disorder in a nonpatient population following exposure to a natural disaster. In this study 469 bushfire volunteer firefighters in Australia had intense exposure to a 1983 disaster and were examined 4, 11, and 29 no. afterward. At 42 no., a subgroup of 147 Ss at high risk for having PTSD was interviewed and found that 70 Ss had PTSD, 44 had an affective disorder and 68 had an anxiety disorder. The use of all the presence of PTSD rather than the absence of symptoms suggested that coping represents a psychological process used to contain the distress caused by symptoms as well as to manage environmental adversity.

Roberts (1995) investigated the applicability of Lazarus and Follman's (1984) goodness - of - fit hypothesis to the relationship between college students with coping daily hassles and psychological symptomatology. Specifically, it is more functional to alter the source of the daily hassle than it is to let the stressor go unchecked and simply try to manage the negative emotions produced by the event. Conversely, given a stressor one can not alter, it is more functional to regulate the emotions produced by the event than to engage in repeated futile attempts to change an uncontrollable stressor. It was predicted that the subject who tended to violate these principles across multiple daily hassles, would be characterized by the highest psychological symptomatology and students positively associated with Psychological symptomatology and students tended to match the method of coping with the appraised controllability of their daily hassles, with no support for the goodness - of - fit hypothesis was found.

Some researches have focused on social support and stress.

Reifman and Dunkel - Schetter (1990) reported a study entitled in which the 'Relationship between college students' social support and social interaction and their health and well-being'. The authors analysed data from a telephone survey of 161 students at a large state university to test for stress buffering and main effects on well-being of four types of structural social support. Frequency of participating in activities with other students was negatively associated with depression symptoms and positively associated with feelings of health and physical fitness. The other support measures yielded less consistent with buffering model interpretations that focus on the role of affectively positive social activities in the well-being of college students.

D'Lurilla and Sheedy (1991) investigated relation between social problem solving ability and subsequent level of psychological stress in college students. A prospective design was used to examine the relation between social problem solving ability and later psychological stress in college students during the first semester of the academic year. A new social problem solving inventory measured not only general ability, but also more specific components of the problem solving process. The results of a hierarchical multiple regression analysis showed that general problem solving ability was negatively related to later stress, even after prior stress level and number of the life problems, were controlled. More specific analysis indicated that subject's problem orientation was a better predictor of stress than their problem solving bills.

Felsten (1991) investigated the effects of situation specific mastery and satisfaction with social support on the appraisal of a situation's stressfulness by 147 male college students. Mastery was positively correlated with the appraisal of desirability of the situation and accounted for 36.9% of the variance. Greater satisfaction with social support was related to more positive appraisals by subjects with high mastery but with more negative appraisals by subjects with low mastery. Mastery and satisfaction with support also interacted to moderate the effects of the number of stressors experienced on total stress. For subjects who faced many stressors, these with low mastery experienced high stress regardless of their satisfaction with support, whereas those with high mastery experienced high stress if their satisfaction with support was low but moderately low stress, if satisfaction with support was high.

Lepore (1992) reported a study entitled 'social conflict, social support and psychological distress : evidence of cross domain buffering effects.' A longitudinal study examined the relative and joint effects of perceived social support and social conflict on psychological distress in 228 college students. Women had higher perceived social support from roommates and friends and less conflict with room mates than did men; there were no gender differences in level of conflict with friends or psychological distress. Room mate conflict predicted increases in psychological distress over time; this effect was attenuated by high level of perceived social support from roommates. These results show the importance of negative and positive aspects of social experience to emotional functioning and the importance of compensatory social support for individuals facing social conflicts.

Lepore *et al* (1993) investigated a study in which social support lowered cardiovascular reactivity to an acute stressor. College students gave a speech in one of three social conditions; alone, in the presence of a supportive confederate, or in the presence of a non supportive confederate. Systolic and diastolic blood pressure were measured at rest, before the speech, and during the speech. While anticipating and delivering their speech, supported and alone subjects exhibited significantly smaller increases in systolic and diastolic blood pressures than did non-supported subjects. Supported subjects also exhibited significantly smaller increases in systolic blood pressure than did alone subjects before and during the speech. Men had higher stress related increases in blood pressures than did women; but gender did not moderate the effects of social support on cardiovascular reactivity. These results provide experimental evidence of potential health benefits of social support during acute stressors.

Lepore (1995) reported a study entitled 'Cynicism, social support and cardiovascular reactivity'. This study examined whether highly cynical individuals benefit less from social support during an acute stressor than individuals low in cynicism. College students (52 men, 52 women) performed a stressful speech task alone or in the presence of a supportive confederate. There was an interactive effect of social support and cynicism on cardiovascular reactivity. But cynicism participants who received support has smaller increase in blood pressure during the speech than low cyicism participants without support and high cynicism participants with or without support. Participants' psychological stress appeared to mediate the main effects of support of blood pressure reactivity, but not the support x-cynicism interaction. Results suggested that cynical attitudes may undermine the stress buffering potential of interpersonal support.

Some other researches have been reported on suicidal thoughts and stress :

Wright (1985) reported a study entitled 'The incidence of serious suicidal thought among 207 high school seniors and 901 college students, and the relationship between serious suicidal thoughts and family stress, drinking and drug abuse problems and delinquency in these groups'. Over 10% of the high school and over 6% of the college students reported ST's. Those considering suicide attempts in both groups were more likely than their classmates to view their parents as having many conflicts with each other, to think of their relationship with their father as poor, to see at least one of their parents as either angry or depressed much of the time, and to perceive themselves as having a drinking or drug abuse problem.

Bonner and Rich (1987) reported a study in which there was a predictive model of suicidal ideation and behaviour from some preliminary data in college students. Within a multivariate statistical design, the relationship of various interpersonal emotional and cognitive variables to suicidal ideation and behaviour in college students was examined. A total of 158 subjects (58 males, 100 females) completed self report measures of life stress, faulty cognitions, loneliness, depression, hopelessness, family cohesiveness, adaptive reasons for living and suicidal ideation and behaviour . The results of a multiple regression analysis, forward-inclusion algorithm, indicated beliefs, and low adaptive reasons for living best accounted for suicidal behaviour scores. To determine the basic structures and power of the predictor variables under study, a factor analysis and composite regression were employed, resulting in a predictive equation consisting of three factors : social or emotional alienation, cognitive distortions, deficient adaptive resources. Results are discussed in terms of an interactional model of suicidal behaviour.

Bonner and Rich (1987) reported a follow-up study to test the concurrent validity of a stress-vulnerability model of suicidal ideation and behaviour. A total of 202 college students (139 females, 63 males) completed self-report measures of life stress, loneliness, depression, disfunctional cognitions, reasons for living, hopelessness, current suicide ideation, and predictions of future suicide probability. The results of multiple regression analysis indicated that 30% of the variation in suicide ideation scores could be accounted for by the linear combination of negative life stress, depressions, loneliness and few reasons for living. The linear combination of current suicide ideation, hopelessness, dysfunctional cognitions, and few reasons for living explained 56% of the variance in self-predicted future suicide probability. The results are interpreted as being supportive of the proposed model.

Bonner and Rich (1988) again reported a study in which an attempt was made to test the predictive validity of a stress vulnerability model of suicide ideation and behaviour. A longitudinal study was conducted with college undergraduates. Measures of social or emotional alienation, adaptive resources for living, and cognitive rigidity were taken at the beginning of the semester and combined to develop a vulnerability score. Then, at mid-term, measures of mid-term stress and cumulative negative life stress were obtained from the some subjects. It was hypothesized that the vulnerability factor would interact with mid-term and negative life stress to predict suicide ideation. Instead of an interactive model a linear, compensatory model of suicide ideation was found. The combination of alienation, deficient adaptive resources, and life stress are best predicted ideation scores.

Garrison (1989) reported a study in which suicidal behaviour was infrequent among school children (12%) but increased progressively among junior high (35%), high school (65%), and college students (50-65%). Though considerable, these values are lower than those of similar age psychiatric population. Estimates of the rate of actual attempt were 3% for elementary students, 11% for high school students, and 15-18% for college students. Most were low-lethality attempts for which medical or other attention was not sought. Accordingly, the vast majority of suicide attempts will not be uncovered by investigations dealing solely with clinical or medically identified populations. The most commonly identified correlates or suicidal behaviours included depressive symptoms, social problems, family disorganization and problems, life stress, and poor, problem-solving skills. Academic problems were not as important.

Jou and Fukada (1997) examined the influence of stress and social support on mental and physical health and happiness of 175 Chinese students enrolled in 13 Japanese Universities. Needed support accounted for only 10% of the variance in reported stress, indicating that the relation between the two variables was not strong and they were generally independent. With greater scores on stress or needed support and lower scores on perceived or received support, depression and somatic complaints become more severe. The higher score on perceived or received support, shows higher happiness. Both perceived and received support showed a buffering effect on somatic complaints. Finally, stress indicating that only among students reporting more stress did students who experienced greater need for support, report more severe depression than those who experienced less need for support.

There were many other studies available in the psychological literature in which efforts had been made to find out the impact of performance and found the impact of performance on stress :

Macknan and Marris (1975), for example, investigated a study of flight crew performance and found that the majority of errors were attributable to deficiencies in group process and not individual proficiency. Finally, group researches proposed that patterns of groups' interaction were effected by environmental factors much as stress.

Marincola and Long (1985) reported another study entitled 'Perceptual style and dual task performance as a function of task difficulty and task emphasis'. The perceptual styles of the 102 subjects were determined by their performance on the Rod and Frame test. Dual-task performance required the subjects to perform concurrently a central tracking task and a peripheral light detection task. The effect of stress on dual-task performance was examined by employing three widely differing levels of tracking task difficulty. Three sets of instruction varied the relative importance of the two tasks within the dual task situation like both manipulation of task within the dual task situation. And both manipulation of task difficulty and instructional set had powerful effects on performance. However, performance differences among subjects with differing perceptual styles were found only on the central taking task with field-independent subjects consistently outperforming field-dependent ones.

Driskell and Olenstead (1989) stated that considerably less is known about the effects of stress on group performance. This is particularly surprising for several reasons. First, the complexity and scope of modern day tasks often require group efforts; second, for these tasks, an understanding of group processes is important for understanding level characteristics.

Harris *et al* (1990) investigated the deleterious effect of stress on human performance. Numerous studies have demonstrâted cognitive behaviour and emotional responses to stress at the individual's level.

Many researches were available on post-traumatic stress :

Vrana and Lauterbach (1994), for example, reported a study entitled 'Prevalence of traumatic events and post-traumatic psychological symptoms in a nonclinical sample of college students'. The lifetime prevalence of traumatic events and their psychological impact were assessed in 440 undergraduate students. Eighty four per cent of the subjects reported experiencing at least one event of sufficient intensity potentially to elicit Post-traumatic Stress Disorder (PTSD). One-third of the sample had experienced four or more traumatic events. Subjects who had experienced trauma reported higher levels of depression, anxiety, and PTSD symptomatology than nontraumatized subjects. These symptoms were more intense in subjects who experienced multiple trauma. Events that were particularly negative in their impact, included unwanted sexual experiences and events, that subjects reported, were too traumatic to discuss openly. Males and females differed in their probability of experiencing some types of events and in the psychological response to certain events.

Silva (1994) reported a study entitled 'Post-traumatic stress disorder : Cross cultural aspects'. This discussed the impact of culture on the incidence and characteristics of post-traumatic disorder. Reaction to natural disorders (e.g. floods, earthquakes) and man-made disorders (e.g. industrial accidents, imprisonment, torture) describe the importance of culture in determining an individual's reactions to stressful situations and in influencing recovery from PTSD is emphasized.

Spurrell *et al* (1994) investigated 'Post-traumatic stress disorder in elderly and younger adults after the 1988 earthquake in Armenia'. The frequency and severity of post-traumatic stress reactions were examined with the relation of exposure, age, sex and death of a family members to these reactions were seen 179 Ss (aged 18-87 years). They were evaluated with post-traumatic stress disorder Reaction Index 1.5 years. after the earthquake. A sub-group of 60 individuals were also assessed for post-traumatic stress disorder with the DSM-III-R. criteria. There was a strong association between the presence of severe symptoms on the index and a DSM-III-R. diagnosis of PTSD. Elderly and younger Ss in cities closer to the epicentre of the earthquake had significantly higher index scores than Ss in more distant location greater rates of chronic severe PSR and were found among highly exposed Ss. Elderly Ss scored higher on arousal symptoms and lower on intrusive symptoms than younger Ss. There was a positive correlation between loss of family members and severity of PSR.

Oswalt and Silberg (1995) reported a study on self-perceived traumatic stress in college students. To evaluate the incidence at college, 179 college students' responses were examined. The analysis indicated that there was a high frequency of self-perceived traumatic stress in this sample; 42% reported traumatic events, whereas only 6% would meet strict diagnostic criteria. Automobile accidents, deaths, and harassment were events perceived as traumatic. Most students turned to themselves or friends for treatment. Apparently traumatic events are more prevalent on campus than previously thought and (with the exception of rape) are rarely covered in prevention programme. College health authorities should be aware of the high incidence of perceived trauma and inform college students of potential stressors to provide appropriate treatment.

Neurotic behaviour : concept

In the psychological literature, the concept of neurosis has been elaborated in general as a form of 'mental disorder'. Neurosis may be considered as the outward and visible sign of an inward and invisible conflict between certain innate tendencies and moral religious prospects imposed upon mind. According to Scheier and Cattell (1961) - 'Neuroticism is sometime defined as those personality characteristics, which actually differ significantly between clinically judged neurotics and normals'.

The neurotic personality may be defined as a basic quality or complex of qualities of traits that leads to over-manifestation of neurosis. Eysenck (1970) characterized neurotic personality as badly organized, schizoid, dyspepsia, poor muscular tone, unsatisfactory homes and cyclothymic. Generally this factor delineates a general lack of personality integration, lack of adaptability and lack of general drive which might justifiably be called neuroticism. Eysenck (1970) has pointed out that there are four independent factors in the psychiatric field, namely (a) Psychoticism (P-factor) (b) Neuroticism (N-factor), (c) Introversion - Extraversion (I-factor) and (d) Intelligence, which is relatively independent of these three but interests with all of them in complex and almost non-neurotic ways.

The psychiatry and medical psychology of contemporary period signifies the concept of neuroticism in a very specified way. Neuroticism is the abstract quality characterising neurosis. Neurosis is the actual disorder while neuroticism is a mild condition of neurosis.

Freud (1920) believed anxiety as the central problem of neurosis. Adler pointed out every 'neurosis can be understood as an attempt to free oneself from a feeling of inferiority in order to gain a feeling of superiority'. Janet believes that neurosis depends on the failure of the individual to adjust himself to life. According to Jung 'neurosis is the result of an act of adaptation that has failed', when the libido is unable to find out-let in the right adaptation it seeks abnormal line of development. Allport defined true neurosis as, stubborn self centredness and he regards that true neurosis is largely dominated by unconscious.

It may be summarised that neurotic implies sensitivity day-dreaming, shyness toward opposite sex, self-consciousness, emotionality, lack of realism, feeling of dependence, lack of initiativeness and enterprise, indecisiveness, inferiority feeling, lack of confidence and courage, unusual anxiety manifested in physical tremor, depression, withdrawal, lack of concentration, nervousness, disturbed sleep (Insomnia), suspicion, pessimism and restlessness. The neurotic is incapable of normal sex life and does have deep sense of praise or blame, thinks life a burden and thinks himself unlucky.

Some other studies reported in the literature on neuroticism would be presented here :

Terry (1986) reported a study entitled 'Caffeine and memory performance on the Auditory Verbal Learning Test'. The Auditory Verbal Learning Test is a memory test that assesses recall of lists of words on single and multiple trials. College students (N = 33) were given the AVLT, either with or without a prior administration of 100 mg. Caffeine. Caffeine subjects recalled fewer words than did control subjects, both after single presentations of lists and across repeated trials. Caffeine subjects showed a greater deficit in recalling the middle-to-end portions of the list. Personality scores on the Mondsley Personality Inventory showed a positive correlation of recall on a pretest with Neuroticism.

Chaudhary and Sinha (1992), for example, examined the effect of extraversion and neuroticism on adjustment in 4 different areas of adjustment : home, health, social and emotional. A sample of 100 male college students participated in the study, which employed the Eysenck Personality Inventory (EPI) and the Bell Adjustment Inventory. Extraversion scores and neuroticism scores were dichotomized into high and low groups. High and low extroverts did not differ significantly in home, health and emotional adjustment. However, high and low extroverts differed significantly in social adjustment : High extroverts showed better social adjustment than did low extroverts. High and low neurotic Ss differed substantially in all four areas of adjustment.

Maguns, *et al* (1993) investigated 4-year longitudinal study of young adults to examine the casual pathways between personality and life events. To reduce measurement artifacts, analyses were conducted using reports of more objective life events. It was found that extraversion predisposed participants to experience more positive objective life events, whereas neuroticism predisposed people to experience more negative objective events. In contrast, personality was somewhat stable, and life events were found not to have a prospective influence on it. Objective, positive and negative life events covaried, suggesting that people who experience more than one type of event are also likely to experience more events of the opposite valence as well. The findings indicated that life events can not be viewed as a source of influence, independent of personality. Although factors that are independent of the person, undoubtfully influence life events to some degree, the personality of the individual also appears to do so.

Christensen *et al* (1993) examined relationship between measures of guilt and shame, embarrassability, self-consciousness, anxiety and personality among 112 undergraduates. Ss scoring, high in neuroticism, as measured by the Eysenck Personality Questionnaire (EPQ), were not troubled by excessive guilt; instead, they were more perfectionistic, anxious, shamed, embarrassed, and self-conscious than were Ss scoring lower in neuroticism. Ss High in neuroticism appeared to believe that they were of sufficient stimulus value to be subject to others close scrutiny.

Cramer (1993) investigated the problem of personality, socio-economic status and age disparity in marriage. The Freudian-derived hypothesis that spouses married to much older partners are more neurotic than spouse married to similarly aged partners, was listed on 1,573 female and 1,455 male White British adults married for the 1st time. The hypothesis was not confirmed in men or women with either the Neuroticism scale of the Eysenck Personality Inventory (EPI) or the 30 items General Health Questionnaire (GHQ). Contrary to findings from a study by Attinson and Glass (1985), greater age disparity in marriage was not associated with lower SES. Extraversion, Neuroticism, and the GHQ were negatively correlated with age disparity for women.

McKenzie and Tindell (1993) examined the relationship between neuroticism, anxiety, and academic achievement in

108 students in a 3rd-year Modular Degree Course. Neuroticism, correlated positively with degree, marks only for Ss with high super ego strength. Correlations between measures of anxiety, obtained by resolving the vector sum of the neuroticism and extraversion scores, show that degree marks were higher than that for neuroticism. Correlations were also higher at degree as opposed to diploma and certificate levels, which suggest that the Furneaux Factor (i.e., a neuroticism-super ego interaction) is more apparent in more academically rigour programmes of study. Results of a zone analysis reveal low negative correlations between verbal ability and achievement for neurotic introverts only and very high positive correlations between verbal ability and degree marks for stable introverts only.

Francis (1993) reported the dual nature of the Eysenckian neuroticism scale. High neuroticism scores were seen for both socially undisturbed and socially unattractive. Females invariably scored higher on neuroticism than males. A new set of data analyses from 191 school students (aged 15-16 years) and 646 undergraduates from the US, UK, and Canada identified two components within Eysenck's neuroticism scales, one of which was sex related and the other sex free. These two components, however, differed from each other in fundamental ways, in addition to their respective relationships with sex, and appeared to measure different aspects of these overall construct of neuroticism.

Mangan *et al* (1993) investigated the relationship between photic driving in the theta, alpha, beta 1, beta 2, and gamma bands and personality dimensions of extraversion (E), neuroticism, (N) and psychoticism (P), obtained from the Eysenck Personality Questionnaire Revised (EPQ-R), was investigated in 34 University students. A principal components analysis of photic driving power at the fouteen frequencies, disclosed four factors : two low, one middle, and one high frequency factor. Although there were no significant relationships between N and photic driving power in any frequency band, P loaded a high frequency (gamma) and E loaded a low frequency (theta) driving factor. It was proposed that more efficient high frequency driving in high Photic power Ss reflected greater cortical strength and that greater theta driving power in extroverts was indicative of an immature nervous system that lacks control over impulsive predispositions.

Torki (1994) investigated correlations between the personality dimensions of extraversion and neuroticism and symptoms of stress reaction during and after the Iraquai invasion of Kuwait in 1990. In total, 225 male and 278 female Kuwait undergraduates were administered an Arabic version of the Eysenck Personality Inventory and a stress reaction ss checklist. The analysis showed no correlation between across one extraversion and stress reaction for men and women during and after the invasion, and a high positive correlation between scores on Neuroticism and stress reactions for men and women during and after the invasion.

Vikem *et al* (1994) did developmental genetic analyses on Extraversion (E) and Neuroticism (N) scale scores from nearly 1500 male and female Finnish twins, ages 18-53 years at baseline. They were tested on two occasions 6 years apart. Significant genetic effect on both traits was found, at all ages, in men and women, on each measurement occasion. For E, heritability was invariant across sex but decreased from late adolescence to the late 20's, with a smaller additional decrease at about 50 years of age. Heritability for N also decreased from late adolescene to late 20's and remained stable thereafter. For all ages after the early 20's, heritability of N was significantly higher among women. Means for E and N were sex dependent and apparently influenced by cohort and time of assessment, as well as by age. There was little evidence of new genetic contributions to individual differences after the age of 30; in contrast, significant new environmental effects emerged at every age.

Irmis (1994) examined whether there was a relationship between EEG results, extraversion and neuroticism. EEG examinations were conducted with 41 neurotic impatients, 27 suicidal inpatients, and 17 healthy controls. All Ss completed the Eysenck Personality Inventory. Ss fell into 4 groups according to the personality inventory scores; high extraversion (HN), neuroticism (LN), and high neuroticism (LN), and LE and LN. No significant indicators of alpha activity and extraversion or neuroticism dimensions were found with the EEG. Also, there were no significant EEG differences among groups - L. Siegmund.

Results of Scheier, *et al* (1994) on depositional optimism, as assessed by the life orientation test (M.F Scheire and C.S. Carver, 1985), had been challenged on the ground, that effects attributed to optimism, were indistinguishable from those of unmeasured third variables, most notably, neuroticism. Data from 4,309 Ss showed that associations between optimism and both depression and aspects of coping remained significant even when the effects of neuroticism, as well as the effects of trait anxiety, self mastery, and self-esteem, were statistically controlled. Thus, the Life Orientation Test did appear to possess adequate predictive and discriminant validity. Examination of the scale on somewhat different grounds, however, did suggest that future applications could benefit from its revision.

Bancroft, *et al* (1994) examined the association of past history of depression and menstrual cycle complaints among women with or without menstrual complaints. Relationship between depressive past histories and current ratings of neuroticism was also examined. In total 90 Ss (aged 20-53 years) with menorrhagia, 83 Ss (aged 17-48 years) with premenstrual syndrome, 50 Ss (aged 19-51 years) with dysmenorrhea and 104 controls (aged 18-56 years), completed the Menstrual Health Questionnaire and the Eysenck Personality Inventory. Past history of depressive illness was most common among Ss with premenstrual syndrome. History of past depression was associated with a tendency for premenstrual depression to be prolonged and with more severe depressive symptoms during premenstrual, menstrual and post-menstrual phases of the cycle. Ss with a depressive history also reported higher neuroticism.

Avila (1994) investigated individual difference in spatial orienting, using a computerized version of M.I. Posuer's noninvasive behavioural paradigm for studying visuospatial attention. In Experiment 1, exogenous facilitation and inhibition of return was measured in 88 undergraduates (aged 18-37 years) grouped according to sensitivity to punishment and sensitivity to Reward Scales. No differences were found for exogenous facilitation between personality groups, but both anxious and impulsive Ss obtained greater inhibition of return than non-anxious and non-impulsive Ss, respectively. In Experiment 2, the same task was administered to 61 undergraduate (aged 18-40 years) classified by extraversion and neuroticism. Neurotic Ss showed more inhibition of return than stable Ss. Findings are consistent with the hypothesis that neurotic and anxious Ss have an attentional system which are more prepared for narrowing attention on locations on immediate relevance.

Gupta and Gupta (1994) examined the effect of caffeine on perceptual judgement. Following a between-subject design, 200 male postgraduate students, classified into 4 personality groups on the basis of their scores on both the neuroticism and extraversion dimensions of Eysenck Personality Inventory, provided data for the study. Four doses of caffeine citrate (1, 2, 3 and 4 mg/kg body weight) and a placebo were used. A double

- blind procedure was adopted for drug administration. Results reveal that (1) caffeine produces differential effects in individuals who presumbly differ in basal arousal, (2) the interaction of neuroticism with extraversion in caffeine effects was significant, and (3) trend components account for differential variation in different personality groups.

Pfeifer and Waclty (1995) examined 44 adult patients with depression, anxiety disorders, and personality disorders. In total 45 healthy adult controls completed a German version of Eysenck Personality Inventory (EPI) and an inventory, measuring extrinsic and instrinsic religiosity and religious attitudes. Beliefs, Neuroticism and religiosity were not correlated. Life satisfaction was correlated negatively with neuroticism and positively with religious commitment. Sexual anxiety, superego conflicts, and childhood fears of God were mainly associated with neuroticism, not with religious commitment. Findings suggested that the primary factor, explaining neurotic functioning in religious patients, is not their personal religious commitment but their underlying pathology.

Berenbaum and Williams (1995) examined the relationship between personality and emotional reactivity. Extraversion and neuroticism were measured using the Eysenck Personality Inventory (EPI). In total, 74 college students were randomly assigned to receive either caffeine or placebo. They reported emotional experience that was measured after Ss viewed positive and negative affect-eliciting film clips, and facial expressiveness was measured from video-tapes recorded while Ss viewed the clips. Facial responses to positive and negative film clips were strongly correlated in both groups. Personality was associated with emotional reactivity among Ss who received placebo but not among Ss who received caffeine. Among Ss who received placebo, higher levels of extraversion were associated with less reactivity to the negative stimuli, and higher levels of neuroticism were associated with less reactivity to positive stimuli.

Reed and Derryberry (1995) assessed differences in 80 undergraduates in response facilitation and inhibition through a modified go/no go task presented in alterating positive and negative incentive blocks. Neurotic extrovert showed enhanced facilitation on positive blocks following positive feedback. Neurotic introverts individuals rated high in State-Trait Anxiety Inventory. Trait anxiety showed enhanced inhibition of negative blocks. Ss, who scored high on the Impulsiveness scale of the 17 Impulsiveness Questionnaire, showed generally low inhibition. Results support models proposing that positive incentive motivation and its facilitatory response consequences peak in neurotic extroverts. However, neurotic introverts were relatively fast in responding following negative feedback, confirming reports of anxious impulsivity.

Ruiz–Caballero and Bermudez (1995) examined the effects of neuroticism of complex personal events from real life. About 45 University students completed the Autobiographical Cognitions Questionnaire, the Eysenck Personality Questionnaire (EPQ) and the Beck Depression Inventory. High levels of neuroticism were associated with a tendency toward fewer happy thoughts and memories. Results also suggest that neuroticism increased retrieval of negative personal memories independent of depressed mood. This tendency to recall negative information appears to play a key role in vulnerability to depression.

Lee *et al* (1995) correlated combat exposure (CE), symptoms of post-traumatic stress disorder (PTSD), and trait eroticism (TN) among 107 veterans. Ss were extensively studied before and immediately after serving overseas in World War II in 1946. Ss were followed by means of biennially mailed questionnaires for 50 years until death. In 1988, 91 Ss completed questionnaires of both PTSD symptoms and TN. Variables, associated with positive psychological health in adolescence and at age 65, years predicted CE and number of psychological symptoms of PTSD in 1946 and 1988. CE also predicted early death and study attrition. Psychological vulnerability in adolescence and at age 65 years and psychological symptoms during civilian stress (but not during combat stress) predicated TN at age 65 years. CE predicted symptoms of PTSD and premortal vulnerability predicted subsequent psychopathology.

Myers *et al* (1995) argued that the Comfort-Discomfort cluster of the Type Differentiation Indicator (a method for scoring Form, J, the research from of the MBTI Myers - Briggs Type Indicator) is not necessarily a measure of the Neuroticism factor of the Five-Factor Model (FFM) of personality. The differences between the goals of the developers of the FFM and those of the developers of the MBTI; differences in the assumptions, principles, practices, and research, associated with the approaches; and the experience of users of the Type Differentiation Indicator are discussed as evidence against the correlation. A cautious perspective is urged in order to avoid erroneous interpretations and minimize potential harm to individuals.

Duggun *et al* (1995) studied the relationship between depressive illness and personality traits from the Eysenck Personality Inventory, using data from a family study. The 1st-degree relatives of probands with major depression (MD) were subdivided into 34 MD recovered relatives, and 45 never ill relatives. Neuroticism and extroversion scores were compared. The relationship between age of onset and recurrence of MD and neuroticism was also examined. Results showed that high neuroticism scores were associated with a past history of MD; there was no such relationship for extraversion scores. Current depressive symptoms were also associated with increased neuroticism score but this did not explain the relationship between previous MD and neuroticism scores. Recurrent episodes of MD in recovered relatives were significantly associated with increased neuroticism scores. It is concluded that high neuroticism scores may be a vulnerability worker for MD.

Mwamwenda (1995) examined the relationship of academic achievement or grade with Eysenck Personality Inventory scores on neuroticism and introversion. About 40 male and 78 female Black South African university students completed the inventory. Contrary to theoretical expectations and previous studies, neither neuroticism nor introversion was related to academic achievement for these Ss.

Walt and Morris (1995) compared performance on a prototype indicator of perceptual defense/vigilance with performance on other related measures of individual differences. On the basis of theoretical expectations and empirical findings, Ss performance on the prototype indicator of perceptual defense or vigilance was predicted to relate to the personality factor of Neuroticism, and to performance on forced-choice extrasensory perceptions (ESP) task. In both the experiments, defensive Ss had higher Neuroticism scores, and lower ESP scores than vigilant Ss. Defensive Ss also consistently showed fewer signs of mental health than vigilant Ss on an exploratory self-report indicator of mental health. Findings indicated that the prototype measure showed some promise as a measure of perceptual defense/vigilance and that with further development it might have a future role in the enhancement of human performance under stress.

Bertolotti *et al* (1995) examined whether anxiety, neuroticism and depression interact with Type A behaviour influenced psychophysiological reactivity in 70 Italian healthy male volunteers (aged 35-59 years). All Ss were blue-collar workers. Cardiac health was confirmed by family/medical history and physical examination. Ss were interviewed and classified as type A or non-type A and assessed for anxiety, neuroticism and depression. Cardiac and electrodermic psychophysiological reactivity were also measured. Results showed that higher neuroticism score in Type A Ss vs a lower score in non-A Ss was associated with greater reactivity. Type A Ss with lower depression scores vs non-A Ss with higher scores had greater cardiovascular responses. No interaction was found between trait anxiety scores and Type A behaviour.

Morris and Robinson (1995) determined if personality neuroticism or extraversion traits were linked to post-stroke depression. A sample of 94 stroke impatient in rehabilitation were examined on post-stroke for presence and severity of depression. A retrospective assessment was made of lifeline neuroticism and extraversion. Results showed that the 35 depressed Ss had higher neuroticism scores than non-depressed Ss. Neuroticism was correlated positively with depressive symptomatology, Extraversion was not associated with depression diagnosis or depressive symptomatology. Personality neuroticism may be a risk factor for depression, following stroke.

Byrne *et al* (1995) prospectively examined stress and smoking onset over 1 year in a cohort of Australian adolescents (aged 13-17 years). In total 1,792 boys and 1,157 girls who were non smokers remained so. A sample of 212 male and 266 female nonsmokers became regular smokers. A sample of 199 boys and 255 girls who were regular smokers remained so. Analysis of data from the Adolescent stress questionnaire yielded a 7-factor structure of stress. Stress of school performance and of future uncertainty were reported by older Ss. Girls reported higher levels of stress than did boys on all factors except those having to do with school attendance and with opposite sex interaction. Neuroticism, as measured by the Eysenck Personality Questionnaire was independently associated with the decision to commence smoking, but did not mediate the association between stress and smoking onset.

Lynn and Martin (1995) examined normative data for extraversion (E), neuroticism (N) and psychoticism (p) and their relationships across 37 nations. National mean scores for E, N and P were obtained with those of work ethic and competitiveness. Data were intercorrelated with additional variables like per capita income and national prevalence rate of suicide, homicide, and alcoholism. Results showed significant relationship between three factor interpreted as E, N and PE had a high loading of 0.55 in P. These results suggested the presence of differing values of the 3 personality dimensions across countries, and of work values like competitiveness and work ethics, and demographic phenomena like suicide and alcoholism, and expressions of these values.

Rehulkova, *et al* (1995) stated that low coping strategies were determined by extraversion and neuroticism. A sample of 309 high school and college students were administered measures of coping strategy and personality. The first factor extracted indicated the coping strategies of express-emotions, wishful thanking, and self criticism as markers of neuroticism. The coping strategy makers for extraversion were problem solving cognitive restructuring social-support and social-withdrawal contrary oriented. It was concluded that neuroticism was associated with coping strategies of the disengagement type, and extraversion with strategies of the engagement type.

Quota *et al* (1995) examined the impact of the Israeli-Palestinian peace treaty and Palestinian children's perception of it on their self esteem and neuroticism. The relative importance of earlier exposure to traumatic experiences and psychological resources in influencing children's psychological well-being after the treaty was also assessed. A total of 64 children (aged 11-12 years) were studied at pre-treaty and post-treaty. Ss traumatic experience, psychological well-being, general intelligence, creativity and political activity were assessed. Results revealed a significant decrease in neuroticism for post-treaty assessment. Acceptance of the treaty and participating in the subsequent festivities mitigated the negative impact of the traumatic experiences on Ss well-being. Increased neuroticism and decreased self-esteem were found only among children who refused to accept the treaty and did not participate in the festivities.

Postgieter and Venter (1995) examined the relationship between adherence to exercise and scores on extraversion and neuroticism. A sample of 116 students and faculty members (mean age 21.5 years) of an academic institution were given a short questionnaire and the Eysenck Personality Inventory (H.J.Eysenck *et al* 1963). When joining a campus exercise facility at the beginning of the academic year 62 Ss, who were still exercising at the gymnasium and 12 more, were classified later as adherers, while those who discontinued were tabled as drop outs in extraversion scores. Drop outs recorded significantly higher neuroticism scores than adherers. It is concluded that there may be an association between psychological well-being and adherence to exercise.

Murray *et al*(1995) investigated the relationship between seasonal affective disorder (SAD) and the trait of neuroticism, as defined by Eysenck (1981), among 258 adult female twins. To investigate the possibility that the dimension of seasonality may not stand alone from nonseasonal mood reactivity, a measure of locus of control of moods was created. Ss were divided into low, middle and high seasonality groups. Results suggested that the tendency to report seasonal variation in SAD symptoms covaries with neuroticism. Furthermore, reports of seasonality were found to covary with a tendency to attribute mood to nonseasonal environmental factors beyond the Ss control. Seasonality scores showed no relationship to extraversion, psychoticism, or to the Eysenck Personality Questionnaire (EPQ) lie scale.

Breslan *et al* (1996) examined an association between migraine and neuroticism. Neuroticism, measured at baseline by the Cysencle Personality Questionnaire, signalled increased risk for first incidence of migraine during a 5 – year follow-up interval. The sample was randomly selected from the list of young adult members of a large health maintenance organization in south-east Michigan. Follow-up data were available on 972 subjects. Neuroticism predicted the first incidence of migraine in females. The relative risk for migraine in female, scoring the highest quartile of the neuroticism scales, versus the lowest quartile was 4.0 (95% CI 1.6,10.3). Controlling for history of major depression and anxiety disorders at baseline reduced the estimate to 2.9 (95% CI 1.1, 7.7). Neuroticism did not predict migraine in males, although the results in males were limited greatly by the small number of cases. Neuroticism might be casually related to migraine, or alternatively, might be an early correlation with shared etiologies.

Kentle (1997) reported a study entitled, 'Elements of neuroticism in relation to headache symptomatology'. The purpose of this study was to ascertain which elements within the factor of Neuroticism are related to headache symptomatology. Consequently, scores on individual items of two neuroticism scales were correlated with headache questions. The first was the Neuroticism scale of Eysenle's Improved short questionnaire which was given along with 20 questions about headache, to 500 university students. The second was the neurotic anxiety scale of the adjective self descriptions scales which was administered, along with 7 questions about headaches , to 400 university undergraduates. Both tension and migraine symptomatology were found to be related to 'tension' items of the neuroticism scales. Migraines were found to be related to cycles of mood. Neither type of headache was found to be especially related to depression. The relationship of headache symptomatology to Neuroticism appears to be slight but direct.

Brown and Moskoitz (1997) examined the relative strength of both affective state and the personality trait neuroticism in predicting common physical symptoms. The authors used an even – sampling design to overcome methodological limitations of past research in the area. Contrary to much previous research, neuroticism was found to be unrelated to reports of physical symptoms, although it was found to be related to unpleasant affective state. Unpleasant affect bore a strong concurrent relation to the frequency of reported symptoms. Temporal relations between experiences of unpleasant effect and subsequent symptoms were found for some individuals, but individual variability was seen in both the strength and direction of this linkage. The findings suggest that when individuals are asked to report their subjective experience of physical illness without the necessity to retrospect over significant period of time, unpleasant effective state is more strongly related to experiences of symptoms than is the trait neuroticism.

Lynn and Martin (1997) investigated Mean gender difference on Eysenck's three personality traits of extraversion, neuroticism, and psychoticism which were collected for 37 nations. Women obtained higher means than men on neuroticism in all countries, and men obtained higher means than women on psychoticism in 34 countries and on extraversion in 30 countries. The relation between the magnitude of the gender differences and per capita income was not significant for any of the three traits.

Gotham, Sher, and Wood (2003) reported a study entitled 'Relations among young adult alcohol use disorders (AUDs), preadulthood (gender, family history, alcoholism, childhood stressors, high school class rank, religion involvements, neuroticism, extraversion, psychotocism) and young adult developmental task (baccalaureate degree completion, full-time employment, marriage)'. Most participants were 424 first-time college students (228 women) who were 18-20 years. Approximately half had a history of paternal alcoholism. Participants were assessed on five occasions over seven years (years 1,2,3,4 and 7). Structural equation modeling suggest preadulthood variables were more salient predictors of developmental tasks that diagnoses, with the majority of effects due to apparent selection. Findings are highly important for prospective multivariate models that specify potential selection, causatio socialization and reciprocal effects in order to fully examine complex relations among young including alcohol involvement, during major life-transition period.

Present Investigation : A Word

Stress is an individualized phenomenon, unique to each person and setting. Pearlin (1989) has suggested that there are two major types of stressors: life events and chronic strains. Life events research considers the extent to which the accumulation of a series of experiences can create a stressful impact. Stress from chronic strain results in role overload: conflicting roles in an individual's life that produce competing, and potentially conflicting demands over time. Role conflict is a common part of the college experience. College students must learn to balance the competing demands of academics, developing new social contacts and being responsible for their personal daily needs (e.g., nutrition and clean clothing). In addition, while the academic workload requires that students face a series of peak periods such as midterms and finals, there is a relatively constant underlying pressure to complete an upcoming assignment.

The transition to college creates a situation where regular contact with traditional supports, e.g., friends from high school and family, may be reduced. The ability of such social supports to mediate the effect of exposure to stress is well documented (Ensel and Lin, 1991; Moss, 1973; Schutt et al. 1994; Thoits, 1995). College marks a period where new systems of social support are being created. This process can, in and of itself, be stressful. Research has shown that events which might otherwise serve to reduce stress, e.g., peer events and social activities, can actually increase feelings of stress during college (Dill and Henley, 1998).

New peer groups that form in college can influence patterns of thought and behavior. Lau et al. (1990) have shown that there is substantial change in the performance of health behaviors during the first three years of college, and those peers can have a strong impact on the types and magnitude of these changes. It seems reasonable, then, that peers may also influence the perception of and reaction to stress. College norms that define certain types of behavior as "appropriate" under certain conditions, e.g., staying up all night to study for an exam, may be stress inducing and may lead to less healthy practices.

Stress has been associated with a variety of negative outcomes in the college girls population including suicide ideation (Hirsch and Ellis, 1996); smoking (Naquin and Gilbert, 1996); and drinking (Morgan, 1997; McCormack, 1996). Research has also documented that females (Megel et al., 1994) and student athletes (Nattiv and Puffer, 1991) are more likely to perceive higher levels of stress. The effects of excess stress on healthy behavior are less well researched within the college-aged population.

It would be evident from the review of the literature on the subject that stress is of paramount importance in the modern world. With advancement in civilization and modernization, an individual's life has become more complex, resulting to stress and neuroticism. It would further be evident that many researches have been conducted in the area of stress and neuroticism. Although the researches are many in the field but they are, by and large, not univocal in nature. In India, many studies of such type are not available. It is needless to mention here that culture and society play an important role in any kind of onset of problematic behaviour. Indian culture is different from that of the western culture in the sense that the inbuilt capacity of Indians provide them shock absorbing capacities. This capacity is expected to result in superior adjustment in comparison to the counterpart of other cultures of the world both in quantity and in quality. An investigation, therefore, on the issue of stress and neuroticism, needed special attention in the Indian context. Researches in India in this direction are still in infancy stage. There is a need to study such problems with more reliable tools and improved methodology. Neuroticism is a personality trait but in the present research the concept of neuroticism has been devoted as the quality of poor mental health. Incidence of poor mental health and stress are not known in India particularly among the student population. Therefore, it is felt as the need of the hour to ascertain the incidence and quality of mental health and stress among college girls. On the basis of the findings of the study, a special cognitive mental health programme can be formulated for the benefit of the Indian population. The present research is, therefore, undertaken to fulfil the same academic and professional need.

3

Methodology

In the previous chapter it has already been dealt upon that there have been enormous studies on this theme. While dealing with the theoretical perspectives of earlier studies, it was felt to look into the dimensions of stress and neurotic behaviour among college girls to pursue their studies in a traditional tour like Varanasi. Hence, the present topic was formulated to pursue the research, keeping in mind the desired methodological issues.

Selection and Formulation of Problem

The problem 'stress and neurotic behaviour in college girls' is selected and formulated for the present study. In order to have detailed information on the topic, relevant journals, periodicals, books and reports were consulted. Many researches have been conducted in the area of stress and neurotic behaviour. It has been found that earlier studies are, by and large, univocal in nature. In India, many studies of such type are not available. Hence, a humble endeavour has been made to investigate the problem at full length leading to specific research in this direction.

Objectives of the Study

The present research was undertaken in those educational institution where high levels of stress are characteristic for much of the student. Rsearcher set out to address three key questions: 1) Are there certain demographic groups who are prone to feel higher levels of stress? 2) Are 'stressed' students more likely to exhibit neurotic behaviour? and 3) Do 'stressed' students exhibit higher levels of neurotic behaviour?

The major aim of the present research was to see the impact of certain psycho-social variables on stress and neurotic behaviour. The specific aims of the study were to:

1. ascertain the influence of curriculum, level of education, caste and economic level of female college students on stress.
2. find out the effect on curriculum, level of education, caste and economic level of female college students on neurotic behaviour.

Hypotheses

The following hypotheses were framed for the study :

(1) The arts and science female college students would differ significantly on their scores on achievement stress scale, academic stress scale, physical stress scale, family stress scale, social stress scale and total stress scale.

(2) The post graduate and under graduate female college students would differ significantly on their scores on SAchS, SAS, SPS, SFS, SSS and total stress scale.

(3) The upper caste and lower caste female college students would differ significantly on their scores on SAchS, SAS, SPS, SFS, SSS and total stress scale.

(4) The high, middle and low economic level female college students would differ significantly on their scores on SAchS, SAS, SPS, SFS, SSS and total stress scale.

(5) The arts and science female college students would differ significantly on their scores on FFA, OBS, PHO, SOM, DEP, HYS, and total MHQ.

(6) The under graduate and post graduate female college students would differ significantly on their scores on FFA, OBS, PHO, SOM, DEP, HYS, and total MHQ.

(7) The upper caste and lower caste female college students would differ significantly on their scores of FFA, OBS, PHO, SOM, DEP, HYS, and total MHQ.

(8) The high, middle and low economic level female college students would differ significantly on their scores on FFA, OBS, PHO, SOM, DEP, HYS and total MHQ.

Instead of above said hypothises it was also hypothisized that -

- There exists relationship between stress and neurotic behaviour.
- Students belonging to lower economic status will be more prone to stress compared to the students of high economic status.
- Students belonging to upper caste will be more optimistic

Research Design

Dependent Variables

(1) Stress

(2) Neurotic Behaviour

Independent Variables

(1) Curriculum (Science and Arts)

(2) Level of Education (Under graduate and Post graduate)

(3) Caste (Upper caste and Lower caste)

(4) Economic level (High, Middle and Low)

Measurement of Variables

In this sections a short description of the psychological test used in the present study for the collection of data and coding of a few items is presented. These scales are briefly described below :

The followings are the main tools (Psychological Tests) employed for the collection of data in the present research :

(i) Bisht Battery of Stress Scale

(ii) Middlesex Hospital Questionnaire

Stress and neurotic behaviour were assessed with the help of Bisht Battery of Stress Scale (Bisht, 1987) and Middlesex Hospital Questionnaire (Crown and Crisp, 1966) respectively. Other relevant details of the subjects were found out through the General Introductory Schedule developed for the purpose.

The details of these tools including the variables which they measure, number of items and range of scores for each test are given in Table 3.1.

Table 3.1 : Description and Details of the Tools

Name of Tools	*Variables*	*No. of Items*	*Range of Scores*
1. General Introductory Schedule	Respondent's Name, Age, Sex, Religion, Caste, Education, Marital Status, Income etc.	9	
2. Bisht Battery of Stress Scale			
	a) Achievement Stress	52	
	b) Academic Stress	80	
	c) Physical Stress	60	0–1436
	d) Social Stress	84	
	e) Family Stress	83	

(Contd.)

(Contd. Table 3.1)

Name of Tools	*Variables*	*No. of Items*	*Range of Scores*
3. Middlesex Hospital Questionnaire	a) FFA	8	
	b) OBS	8	
	c) PHO	8	0–96
	d) SOM	8	
	e) DEP	8	
	f) HYS	8	

The details of the tests used are available in the following paragraphs.

Bisht Battery of Stress Scales (BBSS)

There was a glaring scarcity of tools measuring different types of stresses. Some available tools appeared apparently as measuring some of the types of stress like - Family Questionnaire (Herbart, 1952) which gave a family tension index; Schedule of Recent Experience (Martin, 1983), to measure family stress; Educational Stress Events Inventory (Sharratt, 1983) to measure job related stress; and Stress Scale for School Psychologist (Beirtman 1983). There was of course, availability of tools which measured one or the other components of stress, e.g., anxiety tools were developed by Taylor (1953), Mandler and Sarason (1952), Alpert and Haber (1960), Liebert and Morris (1967), Sinha (1966), Sinha and Sinha (1969), Mc Nair *et al* (1971). But these measures did not suffice the purpose of measuring some exclusive stress type having all the four components of stress, *viz.*, frustration, conflict, pressure and anxiety in them. Therefore, for the measurement of thirteen types of stresses, a 'Battery of Stress Scale' was developed and standardized by Bisht (1987). This Battery had the following scales :

(i) Scale of Existential Stress (SES)
(ii) Scale of Achievement Stress (SAchS)
(iii) Scale of Academic Stress (SAS)
(iv) Scale of Self-Concept Stress (SSCS)
(v) Scale of Self-Actuatization Stress (SSAS)
(vi) Scale of Physical Stress (SPS)
(vii) Scale of Social Stress (SSS)
(viii) Scale of Role Stress (SRS)
(ix) Scale of Institutional Stress (SIS)
(x) Scale of Family Stress (SFS)
(xi) Financial Stress Scale (FSS)
(xii) Scale of Vocational Stress (SVS)
(xiii) Scale of Superstition Stress (SSuS)

All the thirteen scales of the battery were developed and standardized simultaneously. Six approaches were adopted for the standardization purpose, *viz.*

(i) Methodological Approach
(ii) Theoretical Approach
(iii) Static Approach
(iv) Rational Approach
(v) Empirical Approach
(vi) Normative Approach

Methodological Approach

Under this approach a search for a method for measuring stress was done. One method of measuring stress was idiographic, advocated by Vinokur and Selzer (1975), Theorell (1974), Paykel and Uhlenhuth (1972), Andler *et al* (1974). Proclaiming its accuracy, they said. 'It might also reflect the subject's perception as well as his way of coping with life change events'. This widely used method of measuring stress, measured stress through subjective feelings of distress of interpretive perceptual responses. For developing the battery of stress scales this idiographic method was taken.

Theoretical Approach

In this case a five point scale was thought to be appropriate because it took into account the average category into account too. So, for continua were concerned, two continua were taken. One was of frequency along, which items were located in terms of frequency (i.e., always, often, sometimes, rarely, and never) and the other was of quantity along, which items were located in terms of quantity (i.e., very much, much, so, little, and not at all).

Static Approach

Stress was conceptualizatized as having following components:

(a) Frustration
(b) Conflict
(c) Pressure
(d) Anxiety

Rational Approach

Inventories of items in Hindi of different types of stresses were prepared. Inventory items were distributed over the four components of the different types of stresses. Frustration items were based on delays, lack of resources, losses and failures. Conflict items showed three types of conflict - approach - avoidant, double - approach and double avoidance conflicts. Pressure items were on competitive achievement, sustained concentration of efforts, and rapid changes. The worry items of anxiety were on conscious concern about consequences, negative expectation and negative self evaluation. The emotionality items of anxiety were on uneasiness and nervousness.

Empirical Approach

(a) Selection of Items - It was done in a three - fold manner, *viz.*:
    (i) by content analyzing the items

(ii) by knowing the predictive validity of items

(iii) by knowing the discriminatory power of items

(b) Descriptive Statistics - to know the nature of scores by scales, SK and KU were calculated. Reliability of mean, median and SD of scores scored by scales were also chalked out.

c) Determining Psychological Properties of Scales - Four psychological properties of the scales were determined, *viz.*

(i) reliability - reliability of the scales of the battery was calculated in three ways for knowing,

(ii) dependability, i.e., short - term test-retest correlations,

(iii) stability, i.e., retest after longer intervals, and

(iv) internal consistency, i.e., split half correlations.

Dependability, stability and internal consistency (split half) co-efficients of various scale (N=243) were as follows :

Table 3.2 : Co-efficients

Scales	*Dependability*	*Stability*	*Internal consistency*
SIS	0.78	0.73	0.80
SAS	0.87	0.82	0.88
SFS	0.88	0.88	0.62
FSS	0.83	0.72	0.91
SSS	0.77	0.70	0.88
SSuS	0.82	0.78	0.82
SVS	0.90	0.84	0.61
SPS	0.91	0.83	0.78
SScS	0.87	0.84	0.83
SSAS	0.89	0.78	0.90

(Contd.)

(Contd. Table 3.2)

Scales	*Dependability*	*Stability*	*Internal consistency*
SRS	0.78	0.78	0.84
SES	0.79	0.72	0.74
SAchS	0.70	0.66	0.88

(ii) Validity – All the scales appeared to be having content validity and item validity. The method of selecting items supported the supposition. In addition, construct validity (discriminability) was estimated for all scales in a two fold fashion. The first type tested if the construct measured differentiated students on some related construct. For this, memory was taken. The second type tested if the construct measured by the scales were not related to construct predicted by theory. For this, internal evaluation was taken. In both the cases construct validity was affirmed.

(iii) Homogeneity – All the scales were correlated with each other obtained from correlations which were moderate in magnitude, indicating that the scales were measuring one main construct, i.e., stress in general and different types of stresses in particular.

(iv) Transferability – The means of various scale scores of these sample students (100 students of Almora district and one of 100 from Lucknow district) were tested for difference of 't' analysis. The non-significant 't' fairly indicated that items of the scales were not concentrating on one kind of situation and they could be used across different populations.

Normative Approach

Percentile – norms were established for scales of the battery. Normative data were collected from a sample of 300 students. The corresponding grouping of high, average and low stress in terms of percentile for interpretation was –

High stress – P_{70} or above
Average stress – P_{69} to P_{31}
Low stress – P_{30} or below

Scoring

The scoring was as follows for positive statement.

Always Too much	*Often Much*	*Sometimes Average*	*Rarely Less*	*Never Not at all*	*Total*	*Grand Total*
4	3	2	1	0		
4	3	2	1	0		

For negative statements, it was just vice-versa. The total would be separate for frequency and quantity. The grand total would be the sum of frequency score and quantity score. Thus each scale would yield

(a) Frequency of stress score
(b) Quantity of stress score
(c) Total stress score

The items measuring various dimensions of a particular stress in various scales were presented as follows :

Table 3.3 Distribution of items of SAchS (Scale of Achievement Stress) are presented below

Components	*Item Numbers*	
(1) Achievement Frustration	Positive –	2, 4, 8, 10, 15, 16, 21, 25, 28, 33, 36, 37, 40, 41, 44, 46, 51 = 16
	Negative –	32 = 1

(Contd.)

(Contd. Table 3.3)

Components	*Item Numbers*	
(2) Achievement Conflict	Positive –	7, 27, 29, 43 = 4
	Negative –	18 = 1
(3) Achievement Pressure	Positive –	1, 5, 11, 13, 14, 20, 24, 31, 34, 42, 45, 50 = 12
	Negative –	6, 17, 26, 38, 47, 48 = 6
(4) Achievement Anxiety	Positive –	3, 9, 12, 19, 23, 30, 35, 39,, 49, 52 = 10
	Negative –	22 = 1
		Total = 52

Table 3.4 Distribution of items of SAS (Scale of Academic Stress) as follows

Components	*Item Numbers*	
(1) Academic Frustration	Positive –	2, 5, 7, 18, 20, 22, 25, 44, 45, 46, 50, 52, 55, 57, 68, 72, 75, 77 = 18
	Negative –	15, 33, 39, 56, 62, 63, 67, 69 =8
(2) Academic Conflict	Positive –	8, 11, 24, 28, 37, 41, 43, 54, 59, 79 = 10
	Negative –	16, 21, 42, 47, 71 = 5

(Contd.)

(Contd.Table 3.4)

Components	*Item Numbers*	
(3) Academic Pressure	Positive –	1, 4, 14, 23, 26, 31, 32, 35, 38, 58, 60, 61, 70, 73, 76 = 15
	Negative –	3, 6, 10, 29, 34, 53, 64, 74, 78 = 9
(4) Academic Anxiety	Positive –	9, 13, 17, 27, 36, 40, 48, 65, 80 =9
	Negative –	12, 19, 30, 49, 51, 66 = 6
		Total = 80

Table 3.5 Distribution of items of SPS (Scale of Physical Stress) are as follows

Components	*Item Numbers*	
(1) Physical Frustration	Positive –	1, 9, 20, 30, 33, 39, 40, 45, 48, 49, 50, 52, 55, 58, 59 = 15
	Negative –	6, 32, 36, 42, 53, 56, 60 = 7
(2) Physical Conflict	Positive –	7, 17, 41, 57 = 4
	Negative –	46 = 1
(3) Physical Pressure	Positive –	2, 4, 11, 14, 15, 18, 19, 22, 25, 31, 35, 38, 44, 54 = 14
	Negative –	29, 47 = 2

(Contd.)

(Contd. Table 3.5)

Components	*Item Numbers*	
(4) Physical Anxiety	Positive –	3, 5, 10, 12, 13, 21, 23, 24, 27, 28, 34, 37, 43, 51 = 14
	Negative –	8, 16, 26 = 3
		Total – 60

Table 3.6 Distribution of items of SSS (Scale of Social Stress) are as follows

Components	*Item Numbers*	
(1) Social Frustration	Positive –	1, 2, 5, 8, 11, 14, 20, 28, 32, 35, 36, 44, 46, 49, 54, 57, 61, 71, 80, 82 = 20
	Negative –	39, 63, 69, 78 =4
(2) Social Conflict	Positive –	5, 10, 16, 19, 24, 30, 38, 48, 52, 60, 64, 66, 70,72, 74, 77 = 16
	Negative –	68 = 1
(3) Social Pressure	Positive –	4, 17, 21, 25, 27, 29, 34, 40, 43, 50, 55, 58, 76, 79, 81, 83 = 16
	Negative –	9, 31, 33, 53, 67 = 5

(Contd.)

(Contd. Table 3.6)

Components	*Item Numbers*	
(4) Social Anxiety	Positive –	3, 6, 7, 12, 13, 22, 23, 37, 41, 42, 45, 47, 51, 56, 62, 65, 73, 75, 84 = 19
	Negative –	18, 26, 59 = 3
		Total = 84

Table 3.7 Distribution of items of SFS (Scale of Family Stress) are as follows

Components	*Item Numbers*	
(1) Family Frustration	Positive –	4, 5, 7, 12, 22, 25, 28, 35, 38, 46, 47, 50, 51, 59, 69, 82 = 16
	Negative –	2, 11, 15, 20, 40, 49, 57, 83 = 8
(2) Family Conflict	Positive –	8, 10, 16, 29, 41, 44, 54, 58, 60, 65 - 10
	Negative –	6 = 1
(3) Family Pressure	Positive –	1, 14, 18, 19, 27, 31, 36, 42, 43, 45, 48, 52, 55, 56, 66, 68, 74, 77, 79, 80, 81 = 21
	Negative –	17, 24, 26, 32, 37, 61, 67, 70, 76 = 9

(Contd.)

(Contd. Table 3.7)

Components	Item Numbers	
4) Family Anxiety	Positive –	3, 9, 13, 23, 33, 34, 39, 62, 63, 71, 73, 75, 78 = 13
	Negative –	21, 30, 53, 64, 72 = 5
		Total = 83

There were thirteen scales in Bisht Battery of Stress Scale, but only five scales were selected for use in the present study, i.e., Achievement stress, Academic stress, Physical stress, Social stress and Family stress. These were considered more relevant for the college students, hence, selected.

Middlesex Hospital Questionnaire (MHQ)

The Middlesex Hospital Questionnaire (MHQ) is a short, clinical diagnostic self rating scale for psycho-neurotic patients developed by Crown and Crisp (1966). The authors' aim was to get a rapid quantification of common symptoms and traits relevant to the conventional diagnostic categories of neurotic illness and to provide a rapid approximation to what would be expected from a diagnostic psychiatric interview. Instead of simply telling that somebody is more ill than others, the author claimed that the Middlesex Hospital Questionnaire (MHQ) gave a 'quantitative clinical profile'. The test consisted of six sub-scales having eight questions each making a total of 48 questions. The sub-scales are -

(i) FFA – Free Floating Anxiety
(ii) OBS – Obsessive Traits and Symptoms
(iii) PHO – Phobic Anxiety
(iv) SOM – Somatic Concomitants of Anxiety
(v) DEP – Neurotic Depression
(vi) HYS – Hysterical Traits and Symptoms

The test is validated on the following criteria :

1. Each sub-test differentiated the neurotic from the normal at a highly significant level.
2. The sub-test scores correlated with the clinical ratings of the particular diagnostic category.
3. The correlation co-efficients between the sub-tests were moderate to low, showing that they measured different aspects of neurosis but at the same time, all correlations were positive, showing that there was same general underlying factor (i.e. neuroticism) affecting all the sub-scales which could be taken as the neuroticism score.

Since its construction, the MHQ was used by various Psychologists, all of whom demonstrated its superiority over other scales like MPI and PEN (e.g. Cockett, 1969, McKerracher *et al* 1968, Young *et al* 1971, Wolkind and Forrest, 1972).

Further evaluation of the MHQ was done by Crown *et al* (1970), who administered the test to 1208 adult males and provided extensive standardization figures. They came to the conclusion that age and social class could be ignored in normal clinical use and affected the subtests in a varying manner.

Prabhu (1972) used the MHQ (original English form) in the Indian setting and found it to be of the same efficacy as claimed by the original authors. He also found the reliability of each of the sub-tests to be good and the total score of the test to correlate +0.62 with the N scores of the EPI.

A Hindi version of MHQ was adopted by Shrivastava and Bhatt (1973). The Hindi version was prepared by translating the original 48 items of the MHQ (English version) into Hindi.

The hysterical scale, however, was grossly modified. It was infact constructed new, taking into consideration the usual clinical presentation of hysteria in India.

Reliability of the test was calculated by the split half method which was 0.70 by Spearman - Brown formula. The sub-scales reliability co-efficients were found to be -0.88 for FFA

(Free Floating Anxiety), - 0.76 for OBS (Obssesive Traits and Symptoms), - 0.52 for PHO (Phobic Anxiety), -0.68 for SOM (Somatic Concomitants of Anxiety), -0.79 for DEP (Neurotic Depression) and - 0.66 for HYS (Hysterical Traits and Symptoms).

The test was validated against psychiatric patients. It was found that the MHQ scores differentiated the neurotics from the normals at a statistically significant level. The P-value was much less than 0.001 for all the sub-scales. The impaired t-test was used to find the significance of difference.

Table 3.8 Items of each scale are as follows

Sl. No.		*Manifestations*	*Items*
1.	FFA	Free Floating Anxiety	1, 2, 3, 4 and 25, 26, 27, 28.
2.	OBC	Obsessive Traits and Symptoms	5, 6, 7, 8 and 29, 30, 31, 32.
3.	PHO	Phobic Anxiety	9, 10, 11, 12 and 33, 34, 35, 36.
4.	SOM	Somatic Concomitants of Anxiety	13, 14, 15, 16 and 37, 38, 39, 40.
5.	DEP	Neurotic Depression	17,18, 19, 20 and 41, 42, 43, 44.
6.	HYS	Hysterical Traits & Symptoms	21, 22, 23, 24 and 45, 46, 47, 48.

The scoring could be done using the following procedure:

Answers	*Scores*
No, Not at all, Never	o (Except in items 17 and 38 where 'No' score 2)
Yes, Frequently, Very much, Always, Definitely	2 (Except in items 17 and 38 where 'Yes' score 0)
Sometimes, A little, Fairly	1

General Introductory Schedule

Details regarding curriculum, level of education, socio-economic condition and caste were obtained on a schedule, prepared for the purpose. The schedule contained items, relating different variables and the responses obtained by the subjects, were analysed for putting them in various groups required for the purpose.

Sample

A group of subjects selected from the universe for the purpose of obtaining information about that population is called sample. The success of research depends entirely upon the technique of its selection. Various techniques have been devised by the scholars of social science for obtaining a sample, representative of its population. The suitability of a sample depends upon the method used in drawing the sample. Hence, we find that selection of an appropriate sample is of paramount importance in the success of a research scheme.

Keeping in view of the specific purpose of the present study into consideration, the purposive sampling technique has been used. This kind of sampling technique is chosen intentionally because in the light of available evidences purposive sampling technique appears to be suitable for the present investigation, as the researcher intends to study the impact of curriculum, level of education, caste and economic status on the stress and neurotic behaviour of the college girls. Since the subjects for the present study were available without specific planning and difficulties, the technique may be regarded as an incidental technique. Entire selection and estimation are the necessary equipments of the sampling design. It has been tried to present a miniature picture of a cross section of college girls. The total number of respondents were 300. The size of each sample, sub-sample was determined by the number of cases of each classification. It could not be possible to make equal balance in all the groups, because special interest was attached to the difference between more particular stratum.

The sample for the study constituted of 300 unmarried, semi-urban female subjects of normal physical health of Mahatma Gandhi Kashi Vidya Pith University Varanasi (U.P); Udai Pratap College, Varanasi (U.P) and Agrasen Mahajani Post Graduate College, Varanasi (U.P). Only those subjects, who were interested in the research programme, and also, those who had committed themselves for being co-operative for the entire programme were included in the study. The subjects were selected purposively on the basis of curriculum, level of education, caste and economic levels. Of the 300 subjects, 150 subjects belonged to arts group 150 to science group; 150 to under graduate classes, 150 to post graduate classes; 144 belonged to upper caste and 137 to lower caste; 103 to high economic group, 128 to middle economic group and 69 to low economic group. Caste of some subjects could not be clearly located in case of a few subjects of the lot, hence such cases were dropped. The economic level was determined on the basis of income of the subjects. The high income group was of those subjects who full at Q_3 and above of the distribution, the low income group comprised those who were at the below Q_1 of the distribution and the remaining subjects formed the middle income group. The age of the subjects ranged from 17 to 26 years with a mean age of 24.3 years. The distribution of the three hundred sample presented below :

Table 3.9 : Characteristics of the Sample

Variables	*Characteristics*	*Number*
Curriculum	Arts	150
	Science	150

(Contd.)

(Contd. Table 3.9)

Variables	*Characteristics*	*Number*
Level of Education	Undergraduate	150
	Postgraduate	150
Caste	Upper Caste	144
	Lower Caste	137
Economic Level	High	103
	Middle	128
	Low	60

In the present study attempts were made to include as many subjects as well as various settlement. Therefore, the sample size in various subgroups could not be equal because of the non-availability of the desired numbers in the sample.

Procedure

All the previously mentioned tests were administered individually to 300 female college students who belonged to Mahatma Gandhi Kashi Vidya Pith University, Varanasi (U.P.), Udai Pratap College, Varanasi (U.P.) and Agrasen Mahajani PG College, Varanasi. Each female college student was contacted personally. The subjects were explained the purpose of the study. Before administration of the tests, proper rapport was developed with each of the subjects for getting their co-operation during the testing situation. They were told that their responses would be kept confidential. This was done in order to build up a kind of rapport and to get a reliable data.

To the best of efforts, the subjects were tested in the informal situation in their natural and normal psychological environment. In spite of all these precautions and arrangements, there were cases of drop outs (experimental mortality) mostly due to incomplete testing. Each subjects's responses were scored according to the scoring system prescribed for different test. At the end of the test administration the subjects were complemented with thanks for being patient and co-operative. This, has, otherwise, helped the researcher to pursue the research with ease and reliability of the data.

Lastly, comparisons were made among the different groups in order to find out the difference on various aspects of stress and neurotic behaviour by using appropriate and suitable statistical techniques.

Plan of Analysis

The main objective of the present study is to find out the influence of curriculum, level of education, caste and economic status of female college students on stress and to find out the effect of curriculum, level of education, caste and economic level of female college students on neurotic behviour.

It was planned to compute the t-test of significance , where there were only two groups and the ANOVA was used where there were more than two groups. If 't' & 'F' value is greater than the corresponding value of 't' & 'F' ratio, in such cases, it is significant at 0.05 level, the sample mean scores were considered to differ significantly. Analysis and interpretation of the data is presented in Chapter-4.

4

Analysis and Interpretation of Data

The data were tabulated, classified and analysed according to the aims of the present study and were put in the tabular form. This provided necessary information to interpret the existing facts. As said earlier, the data for the present study were collected from the female college students. Specific tools were administered on the subjects to measure the stress and neurotic behaviour. The Bisht Battery of Stress Scale was used in the present study for the measurement of stress and the Middlesex Hospital Questionnaire was used for the measurement of neurotic behaviour.

Thus, the data obtained were analysed in relation to the following main objectives in view :

- to ascertain the influence of curriculum, level of education, caste and economic level of female college students on stress
- to find out the effect of curriculum, level of education, caste and economic level of female college students on neurotic behaviour

The data obtained on different independent variables *viz.*, curriculum, level of education, caste and economic status on the Bisht Battery of Stress Scale were analysed adapting t – test and F – test of significant. Curriculum had two groups – arts and science; level of education had two groups – under

Graduate and Post Graduate, caste had two groups –upper caste and lower caste and economic status had three groups – high, middle and low. The t – test of significance was used where there were only two groups and the ANOVA was used where there were three groups. The dependent variable stress, had five areas and one total status. The stress scores in each scale can be interpreted as (i) Total frequency stress (ii) Total quantity of stress and (iii) Total amount of stress (it is the sum total of frequency scores and quantity scores). Thus in this way, such analysis was done on six dependent variable scores. The measurement was done with the help of the Bisht Battery of Stress Scale.

Demographics: Stress and Neurotic Behaviour

The demographic attributes of student respondents has been reported in Table 4.1 – 4.4.

Table 4.1 Student Respondent and Curriculum Demographics

Curriculum	*Sample N*	*Sample %*
Arts	150	50
Science	150	50
TOTAL	300	100

Table 4.2 Student Respondent and Level of Education Demographics

Level of Education	*Sample N*	*Sample %*
Undergraduate	150	50
Postgraduate	150	50
TOTAL	300	100

Table 4 .3 Student Respondent and Caste Demographics

Caste	*Sample N*	*Sample %*
Upper Caste	144	48
Lower Caste	137	45.6
TOTAL	181	93.33

(*) NOTE: Ninteen respondents failed to indicate a caste category, and were treated as "missing" cases in terms of their caste.

Table 4.4 Student Respondent and Economic Status Demographics

Socio-economic Status	*Sample N*	*Sample %*
High	1033	4.3
Middle	1284	2.6
Low	60	20
TOTAL	300	100

Most students (52.1%) indicated relatively high levels of stress during the course of a "typical semester."

The three hundred unmarried semi-urban female college students of normal physical and mental health have been considered as sample for the present study. The data were collected from different educational institutions of Varanasi City of Uttar Pradesh. It is reflected from above table(s) 4.1 to 4.4 that 50% (N=150) subjects belonged to arts group and rest of the 50%(N=150) belonged to science group. The 50% of the total sample were taken from under graduate classes and 50% from post graduate classes. The respondents were predominantly from middle economic status (42.6%,

N=128),whereas 34.3% (N=103) belonged to high economic status and rest of the 20% (N=60) belonged to low economic status.The majority of respondents (48%, N=144) belonged to so called upper caste with a relatively mix of lower caste (45.6%, N=137).

The outcome of analysis of arts and science female college students on the frequency, quantity and total achievement stress has been assessed in Table –4.5.

Table 4.5 Mean comparisons of arts and science female college students on the frequency, quantity and total achievement stress

Components	*Groups compared*	*N*	*Mean*	*SD*	*t*
Frequency of Achievement Stress	Science	150	144.6	28.29	2.94 **
	Arts	150	135.5	25.17	
Quantity of Achievement Stress	Science	150	95.90	30.31	5.90 **
	Arts	150	76.83	25.39	
Total Achievement Stress	Science	150	287.83	54.47	2.63 **
	Arts	150	271.83	47.47	

*** Significant at 0.01 level.*

A perusal of Table-4.5 revealed that the mean difference of arts and science female college students on the frequency, quantity and total achievement stress is differ significantly when compared between the two means. The obtained t- values are 2.94, 5.90, 2.63 respectively with 298 df. The mean values of science students are higher than those of arts students. The mean values of both the group *viz.*, science and arts, are 144.6, 95.90, 287.83 and 135.5, 76.83, 271.83 respectively with 28.29, 25.39, 57.47 and 25.17, 25.39 & 47.47 SDs. The difference regarding the frequency, quantity and total achievement stress is found to be statistically significant at 0.01 level of confidence.

It may be recalled that the first hypothesis formulated in the present research in Chapter 3 is that science and arts female college students may differ significantly. The hypothesis is confirmed in the present research. The global view can be ascertained easily on the basis of graphical representation of data (Fig. 5).

The findings can be rationalized by their better career scope and expectations regarding achievement from their family and society as well as in case of the science students. However, the social background of the family set-up in case of the arts students less motivate them in general.

A comparison of mean values of science and arts college girls on the frequency quantity and total academic stress has been reported in Table-4.6.

Table 4.6 Mean comparisons of science and arts college girls on the frequency, quantity and total academic stress

Components	*Groups compared*	*N*	*Mean*	*SD*	*t*
Frequency of Achievement Stress	Science	150	144.6	28.29	2.94 **
	Arts	150	135.5	25.17	
Quantity of Achievement	Science	150	95.90	30.31	5.90 **

(Contd.)

(Contd. Table 4.6)

Components	*Groups compared*	*N*	*Mean*	*SD*	*t*
Stress	Arts	150	76.83	25.39	
Total	Science	150	287.83	54.47	
Achievement					2.63 **
Stress	Arts	150	271.83	47.47	

*** Significant at 0.01 level.*
NS Not significant

The Table 4.6 compares the frequency quantity and total academic stress of science and arts college girls. The data presented in this table reveal that science and arts college girls differ significantly only on the frequency of academic stress, (t = 5.45 df 298 p < .01). The two groups do not differ significantly on their scores on quantity of academic stress and total academic stress. Although the difference between science and arts college girls are statistically not significant but it may be noted that science college girls have obtained higher scores on quantity of academic stress and total academic stress scale than arts college girls. It was hypothesized that science and arts college girls would differ significantly. Here, in this study, it is partially accepted. The graph in Fig. 5 depicts the above mentioned trend clearly.

The findings can also be justified in terms of better academic level in family and its expectations from the science students regarding the academic success.

The outcome of analysis of arts and science college girls on the frequency, quantity and total physical stress available in Table 4.7.

Table 4.7 The mean comparisons of arts and science college girls on the frequency, quantity and total physical stress.

Components	*Groups compared*	*N*	*Mean*	*SD*	*t*
Frequency of	Arts	150	202.03	48.86	
Physical					205 NS
Stress	Science	150	201.00	37.35	
Quantity of	Arts	150	145.97	28.64	
Physical					3.78 NS
Stress	Science	150	134.17	25.39	
Total	Arts	150	344.76	60.77	
Physical					1.20 NS
Stress	Science	150	336.83	53.25	

NS Not significant

A comparison has been made in Table 4.7 between arts and science college girls on the frequency, quantity and total physical stress. The result gives a clear indication that none of the three comparisons shows any significant difference between arts and science college girls on this measure.

Although, there exists statistically insignificant difference between arts and science college girls on the frequency, quantity and total physical stress, but it may be noted that arts college girls tends to have slightly higher mean scores on the frequency, quantity and total physical stress in comparison to science college girls. Thus the hypothesis formulated in this connection that arts and science college girls may differ significantly on their scores on the frequency, quantity and total physical stress is rejected in the present study. The result is further illustrated through the graph in Fig. 5.

Physical stress among both the science and arts students have been found to be almost of equal level perhaps because there is no significant role of the curriculum.

The outcome of analysis of arts and science college girls on the frequency, quantity and total social stress has been assessed in Table – 4.8.

Table 4.8 Mean comparisons of arts and science college girls on the frequency, quantity and total social stress

Components	*Groups compared*	*N*	*Mean*	*SD*	*t*
Frequency of Social Stress	Arts	150	128.61	38.79	5.20**
	Science	150	107.17	24.81	
Quantity of Social Stress	Arts	150	138.10	44.88	5.69 **
	Science	150	113.83	26.76	
Total Social Stress	Arts	150	270.50	83.82	5.76 **
	Science	150	223.82	53.44	

*** Significant at 0.01 level*

The Table 4.8 presents comparisons of arts and science college girls on the frequency, quantity and total social stress. A look into table reveals that the comparisons indicate significant differences between the mean scores of arts and science college girls. The obtained t – values are 5.20, 5.69 and 5.76 respectively with 298 df. The two groups however, differ significantly at 1% level of confidence. The arts college girls have higher mean values. Thus, it is evident from the result

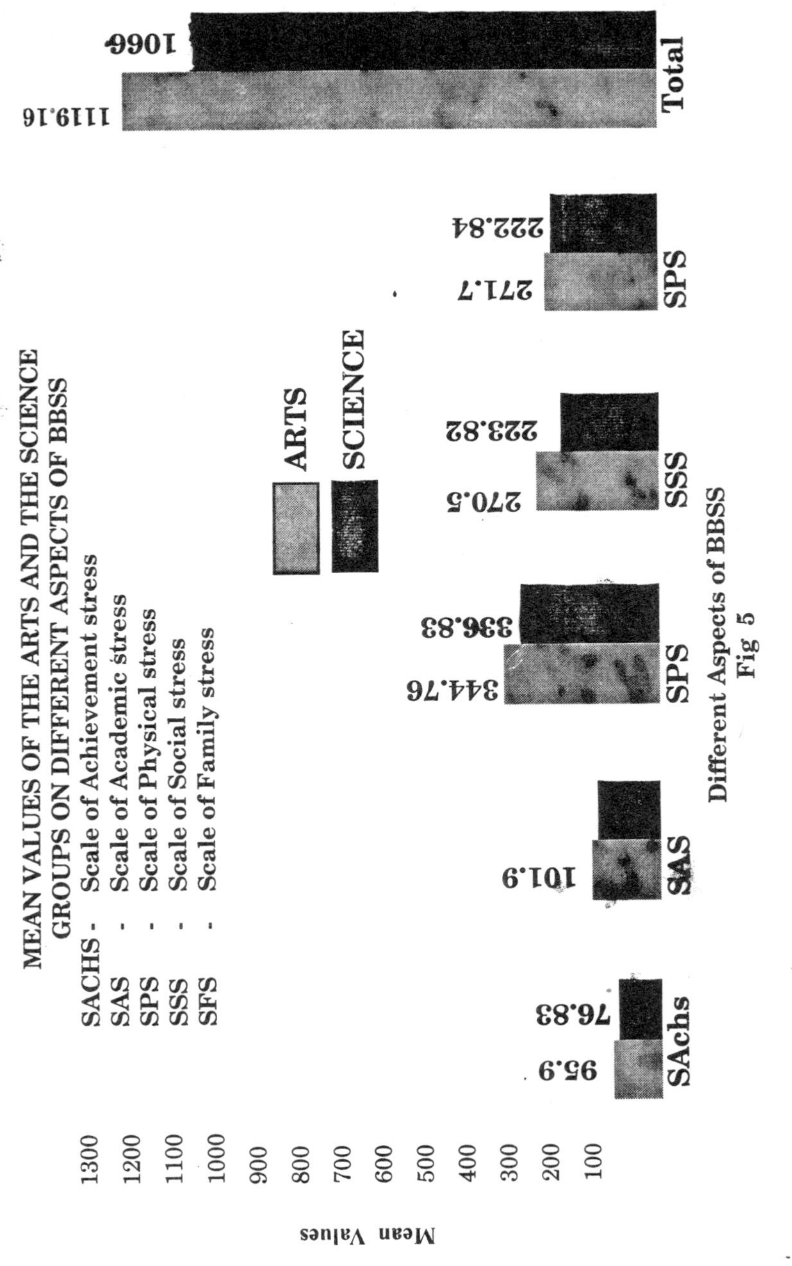
MEAN VALUES OF THE ARTS AND THE SCIENCE GROUPS ON DIFFERENT ASPECTS OF BBSS
SACHS - Scale of Achievement stress
SAS - Scale of Academic stress
SPS - Scale of Physical stress
SSS - Scale of Social stress
SFS - Scale of Family stress
ARTS
SCIENCE
Mean Values
1300
1200
1100
1000
900
800
700
600
500
400
300
200
100
95.9
76.83
SAchs
101.9
SAS
344.76
336.83
SPS
270.5
223.82
SSS
271.7
222.84
SPS
1119.16
1066
Total
Different Aspects of BBSS

Fig 5

that arts college girls have greater social stress. The hypothesis formulated in this connection is therefore proved. A look into Fig. 5 confirms the above trends.

The higher level of social stress among the arts students can be attributed to various social constrains regarding their inferior social status. Generally people think that the students, who choose arts group are less intelligent than science groups.

A comparison of mean values of arts and science college girls on the frequency, quantity and total family stress has been assessed in Table – 4.9

Table 4.9 Mean comparisons of arts and science college girls on the frequency, quantity and the total family stress.

Components	*Groups compared*	*N*	*Mean*	*SD*	*t*
Frequency of Family Stress	Arts	150	131.17	35.61	2.20 *
	Science	150	103.17	31.98	
Quantity of Family Stress	Arts	150	139.77	39.89	3.48 **
	Science	150	115.83	36.67	
Total Family Stress	Arts	150	271.70	75.79	5.97 **
	Science	150	222.84	65.65	

*** Significant at 0.01 level*

** Significant at 0.05 level*

The Table 4.9 shows the comparison of mean scores of arts and science college girls on the frequency, quantity and total family stress. Mean values of the arts and science college girls on the frequency, quantity and total family stress are

131.17, 103.17, 139.77, 115.83, 271.70 and 222.84 respectively with 35.61, 31.98, 39.89, 36.67, 75.79 and 65.65 SDs. All the t-values, as reflected in the Table (2.20, 3.48 and 5.97 with 298 df), reveal that there is a significant difference between arts and science college girls on the frequency, quantity and total family stress. The arts college girls obtained higher mean values. Thus, it is evident from the result that the arts college girls have more family stress than science college girls. The hypothesis formulated in this connection is therefore proved. The tendency is well reflected in the graph as shown in Fig. 5.

The findings can also be justified in terms of family stress, which has been found higher among the arts students and can be attributed to inferior status in family.

A comparison of mean values of arts and science college girls on the frequency, quantity of total stress and total stress has been given in Table – 4.10.

Table 4.10 Mean comparisons of arts and science college girls on the frequency, quantity of total stress and grand total stress

Components	*Groups compared*	*N*	*Mean*	*SD*	*t*
Frequency of Total Stress	Arts	150	611.83	1.34.21	6.46 **
	Science	150	523.83	98.89	
Quantity of Total Stress	Arts	150	615.83	139.52	2.45 *
	Science	150	580.50	107.70	
Grand Total	Arts	150	1222.17	269.86	5.65 **

(Contd.)

(Contd. Table 4.10)

Components	*Groups compared*	*N*	*Mean*	*SD*	*t*
Stress	Science	150	1066.17	202.79	

*** Significant at 0.01 level*
** Significant at 0.05 level*

In Table 4.10 a comparison between arts and science college girls is made on the scores obtained from the frequency of total stress, quantity of total stress and grand total stress. The difference between the mean values in two groups has been found to be statistically significant t = 6.46, 2.45 and 5.65 respectively on the frequency of total stress, quantity of total stress and grand total stress. It may be noted that the arts college girls have higher mean scores than science college girls. Thus, it is evident from the result that the arts college girls are found to be more stressed than science college girls. Thus, the hypothesis formulated in this connection is accepted in the present study. It was hypothesized that arts and science college girls would differ significantly on their scores on the frequency of total stress, quantity of total stress and grand total stress. The total picture has been depicted very clearly by the graph in Fig. 5.

However, total stress among the arts students is higher than science students because of the fact that arts students get less family support as well as social status in terms of less job opportunity, as reported by the arts students.

On the basis of findings of study of two groups *viz.*, arts and science students on various aspects of the BBSS, following conclusions might be drawn :

1. The two groups in question *viz.*, the arts and science college girls did differ significantly on the frequency, quantity and total achievement stress; frequency of academic stress; frequency, quantity and total social stress; frequency, quantity and total family stress; frequency of total stress, quantity of total stress and grand total stress. The arts students have higher mean values than thoes of the science students.
2. The two groups, in question, however, did not differ significantly on the quantity of academic stress, total academic stress; frequency, quantity of physical stress and total physical stress.

Similar type of analysis was done for the scores obtained on various aspects of BBSS by the two groups *viz.*, under graduate and post graduate college girls. The outcome of such analysis is available in Tables – 4.11 - 4.16.

The outcome of the analysis of the post graduate and under graduate college girls on the frequency, quantity and total achievement stress has been reported in Table 4.11.

Table 4.11 Mean comparisons of post graduate and under graduate college girls on the frequency, quantity and total achievement stress

Components	*Groups compared*	*N*	*Mean*	*SD*	*t*
Frequency of Achievement Stress	Post Graduate	150	99.77	24.14	2.25 *
	Under Graduate	150	94.50	15.52	
Quantity of Achievement Stress	Post Graduate	150	101.90	25.05	2.22 *
	Under Graduate	150	96.17	19.45	
Total Achievement Stress	Post Graduate	150	202.03	48.86	2.16 *
	Under Graduate	150	191.17	87.35	

** Significant at 0.05 level*

A look into the Table – 4.11 reveals that the mean difference of post graduate and under graduate college girls on the frequency, quantity and total achievement stress differs significantly when compared between the two means. The obtained t -values are 2.25, 2.22 and 2.16 respectively with 298 df. The mean values of the post graduate college girls are higher than of under graduate college girls. The mean values of the groups *viz.*, post graduate and under graduate college girls are 99.77 and 94.50, 101.90, 96.17, 202.03 and 191.17 respectively with 24.14, 15.52, 25.05, 19.45 and 48.86 and 37.35 SDs. The difference regarding the frequency, quantity and total achievement stress is found to be statistically significant at 0.05 level of confidence. It was hypothesized that post graduate and under graduate college girls would differ significantly on their scores on frequency, quantity and total achievement stress is confirmed in the present research. The global view can be ascertained easily on the basis of graphical representations of data in Fig. 6.

The achievement stress score of post graduate students has been found to be higher than under graduate students. This finding can be rationalized due to the fact that post graduate students are more anxious to achieve economic self-sufficiency for their better future and career.

The outcome of analysis of the post graduate and the under graduate college girls on the frequency, quantity and total academic stress is available in Table – 4.12.

Table 4.12 Mean comparisons of post graduate and under graduate college girls on the frequency, quantity and total academic stress

Components	*Groups compared*	*N*	*Mean*	*SD*	*t*
Frequency of Academic	Post Graduate	150	145.64	28.64	3.78 **

(Contd.)

(Contd.Table 4.12)

Components	*Groups compared*	*N*	*Mean*	*SD*	*t*
Stress	Under Graduate	150	134.17	25.39	
Quantity of	Post Graduate	150	144.60	28.29	2.94 *
Academic					
Stress	Under Graduate	150	135.50	25.17	
Total	Post Graduate	150	282.93	57.47	1.99 *
Academic					
Stress	Under Graduate	150	270.83	47.47	

*** Significant at .01 level*
** Significant at .05 level*

The Table – 4.12 presents comparisons of the post graduate and the under graduate college girls on the frequency, quantity and the total academic stress. Means and standard deviations of the frequency, quantity and the academic stress for post graduate and the under graduate college girls have been presented in the table along with 't' values. A look into the table reveals that the comparisons indicate significant difference between the mean scores of post graduate and under graduate college girls. The obtained t-values are 3.78, 2.94 and 1.99 respectively with 298 df. The two groups, however, differ significantly at 0.01 and 0.05 level of confidence. The post graduate college girls have higher mean values. Thus, it is evident from the result that the post graduate college girls have greater academic stress. The hypothesis formulated in this connection is therefore proved. A look into the graph in the figure 6. Confirms the above trend.

Academic stress score of the post graduate students has also been found to be higher than under graduate students. This finding can also be rationalized due to anxiety for the academic success.

A comparison of mean values of post graduate and under graduate college girls on the frequency, quantity and total physical stress is available in Table – 4.13.

Table 4.13 Mean comparison of post graduate and under graduate college girls on the frequency, quantity and total physical stress

Components	*Groups compared*	*N*	*Mean*	*SD*	*t*
Frequency of Physical Stress	Post Graduate	150	91.83	30.39	2.02 *
	Under Graduate	150	98.09	30.31	
Quantity of Physical Stress	Post Graduate	150	95.17	32.56	2.05 *
	Under Graduate	150	102.37	33.29	
Total Physical Stress	Post Graduate	150	186.03	63.25	2.05 *
	Under Grduate	150	199.76	60.77	

** Significant at 0.05 level*

Table – 4.13 compares the frequency, quantity and total physical stress of post graduate and under graduate college girls. The data presented in this table reveal that the post graduate and under graduate college girls differ significantly on the frequency, quantity and total physical stress (t=2.02, 2.05 and 2.05 df = 298 P < 0.05). It may be noted that the under graduate college girls have higher mean values than post graduate college girls on their scores on the frequency quantity and total physical stress. It means under graduate college girls have more physical stress than post graduate college girls. Thus the hypothesis formulated in this connection that post graduate and under graduate college girls would differ significantly on their scores on the frequency, quantity and total physical stress, is accepted in the present study. The result is further illustrated through the graph in Fig. 6.

This finding can be rationalized due to the fact that under graduate students have just crossed the adolescence period and entered into the next adult phase of life so that they are more anxious regarding their external outlook but neither much concerned about their career nor they are concerned with their future.

The outcome of analysis of post graduate and under graduate college girls on the frequency, quantity and total social stress is available in Table – 4.14.

Table 4.14 Mean comparisons of post graduate and under graduate college girls on the frequency quantity and total social stress

Components	*Groups compared*	*N*	*Mean*	*SD*	*t*
Frequency of Social	Post Graduate	150	131.17	35.61	2.08 *
Stress	Under Graduate	150	122.17	38.98	
Quantity of Social	Post Graduate	150	139.77	39.89	2.32 *
Stress	Under Graduate	150	128.83	41.67	
Total Social	Post Graduate	150	270.71	75.79	2.11 *
Stress	Under Graduate	150	251.84	78.56	

** Significant at 0.05 level*

Table 4.14 presents comparisons between post graduate and under graduate college girls on the frequency, quantity and total social stress. Means and standard deviations of social stress scores for the post graduate and under graduate college girls have been presented in the table along with 't' values. A look into table reveals that the comparisons indicate significant difference between the means scores of post graduate and under graduate college girls. The obtained t-values are 2.08, 2.32 and 2.11 respectively with 298 df. The two groups, however, differ statistically which is significant at 5% level of confidence. The post graduate college girls have higher mean values. Thus, it is evident from the result that the graduate college girls have more social stress than under graduate college girls. The hypothesis formulated in this connection is therefore proved. A look into the graph in Fig. 6 confirms the above trend.

The finding can be rationalized due to more expectation from the post graduate students regarding their establishment in terms of economic stability as well as to bear the burden of family responsibility.

A comparison of mean values of post graduate and under graduate college girls on the frequency, quantity and total family stress is reported in Table – 4.15.

Table 4.15 Mean comparisons of post graduate and under graduate college girls on the frequency, quantity and total family stress

Components	*Groups compared*	*N*	*Mean*	*SD*	*t*
Frequency of Family	Post Graduate	150	128.60	38.79	2.80*

(Contd.)

(Contd. Table 4.15)

Components	*Groups compared*	*N*	*Mean*	*SD*	*t*
Stress	Under Graduate	150	117.83	26.68	
Quantity of Family	Post Graduate	150	138.10	44.88	3.28**
Stress	Under Graduate	150	123.83	28.86	
Total Family	Post Graduate	150	270.50	83.62	3.20**
Stress	Under Graduate	150	243.82	58.44	

*** Significant at 0.01 level*
** Significant at 0.05 level*

The Table 4.15 shows the comparisons of post graduate college girls and under graduate college girls on the frequency, quantity and total family stress. The mean values of both the groups *viz.*, post graduate and under graduate college girls on the frequency, quantity and total family stress are 128.60 and 117.83, 138.10, 123.83, 270.50 and 243.82 respectively with 38.79, 26.68, 44.88, 28.86, 83.62 and 58.44 SDs. All the t-values as reflected in the Table (2.80, 3.28 and 3.20 with 298 df) reveal that there is a significant difference between post graduate and under graduate college girls on the frequency, quantity and total family stress. The post graduate college girls have higher mean values. Thus, it is evident from the result that post graduate college girls have more family stress than under graduate college girls. The hypothesis formulated in this connection is therefore totally accepted. The tendency is well reflected in the graph shown in Fig. 6.

This finding can also be rationalized due to the indirect pressure from parents and other family members to take the responsibility of themselves and family in future as a whole.

The outcome of analysis of post graduate and under graduate college girls on the frequency, quantity and total stress has been presented in Table –4.16.

Table 4.16 Mean comparisons of post graduate and under graduate college girls on the frequency quantity of total stress andgrandtotal stress

Components	*Groups compared*	*N*	*Mean*	*SD*	*t*
Frequency of Total Stress	Post Graduate	150	599.94	157.37	2.85 **
	Under Graduate	150	551.37	136.78	
Quantity of Total Stress	Post Graduate	150	619.54	169.67	2.87 **
	Under Graduate	150	566.17	148.34	
Total Stress	Post Graduate	150	1218.99	309.24	2.90 **
	Under Graduate	150	1119.16	285.33	

*** Significant at 0.01 level*

In Table 4.16 a comparisons between post graduate and under graduate college girls is made on the scores obtained from the frequency, quantity of total stress and grand total stress. The difference between the two groups *viz.*, post graduate and under graduate college girls has been found to be statistically significant t = 2.85, 2.87 and 2.90 respectively on the frequency of total stress, quantity of total stress and grand total stress. It may be noted that post graduate college

MEAN VALUES OF POST GRADUATE & UNDER GRADUATE GROUPS ON DIFFERENT ASPECTS OF BBSS

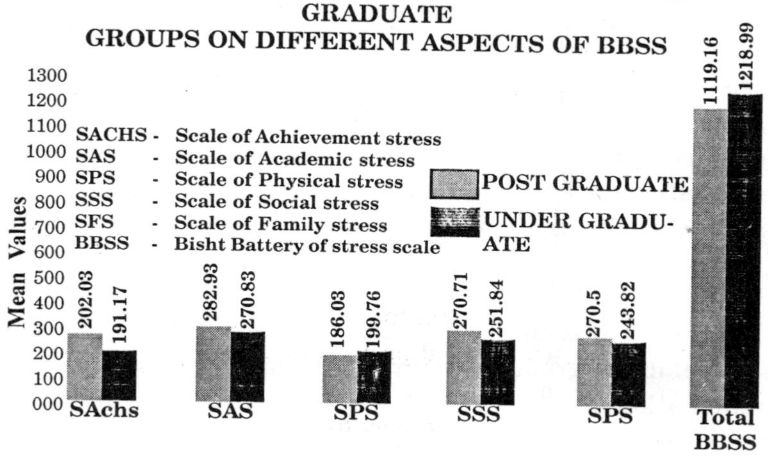

Different Aspects of BBSS

Fig. 6

MEAN VALUES OF ARTS UNDERGRADUATE, SCIENCE UNDER GRADUATE AND ARTS POST GRADUATE, SCIENCE POST GRADUATE GROUPS ON DIFFERENT ASPECTS OF BBSS

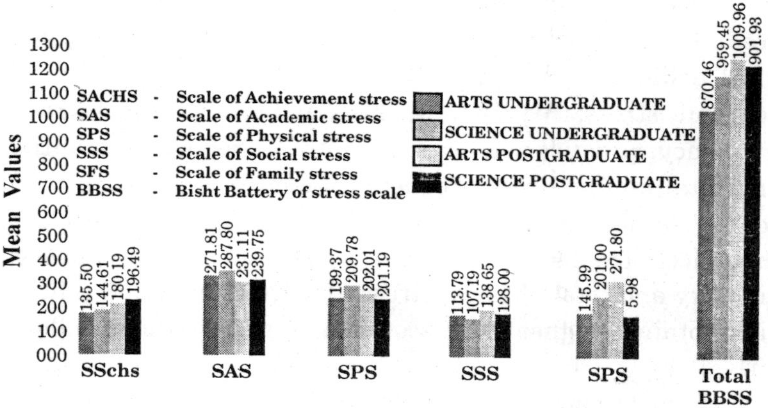

Different Aspects of BBSS

Fig. 7

girls have higher mean values than under graduate college girls. Thus, it is evident from the result that post graduate college girls are found to be more stressed than under graduate college girls. Thus, the hypothesis formulated in this connection is accepted in the present study. It was hypothesized that post graduate and under graduate college girls would differ significantly on their scores on the frequency, quantity, and total stress. The total picture has been depicted very clearly in Fig. 6.

Fig. 7 presents a graphic representation of arts and science, under graduate and post graduate groups in various combinations.

The higher level of stress among the post graduate students can be attributed to more pressure of family as well as society regarding their establishment in terms of economic self-sufficiency. They themselves are also more anxious for their career and future, as reported by the subject.

On the basis of findings of study, two groups *viz.*, under graduate and post graduate on various aspects of BBSS following conclusions can be drawn :

The two groups in question *viz.*, under graduate and post graduate did differ significantly on the frequency, quantity and total achievement stress; frequency, quantity and total academic stress; frequency, quantity and total physical stress; frequency, quantity and total social stress; frequency, quantity and total family stress; frequency; quantity and grand total stress; The post graduate college girls have higher mean values than thoes of under graduate college girls. But on the frequency, quantity and total physical stress, the under graduate college girls obtained higher mean scores than post graduate college girls.

Similar kind of analysis was done for the scores obtained on various aspects of BBSS by the two groups *viz.*, upper caste and lower caste college girls. The outcome of such analysis is available in Table 4.17 - 4.22.

The outcome of the analysis of the upper caste and lower caste college girls on the frequency, quantity and total achievement stress is available in Table – 4.17.

Table 4.17 Mean comparisons of upper caste and lower caste college girls on the frequency, quantity and total achievement stress

Components	*Groups compared*	*N*	*Mean*	*SD*	*t*
Frequency of Achievement	Upper Caste	144	104.77	25.14	3.58 **
Stress	Lower Caste	137	95.98	14.91	
Quantity of Achievement	Upper Caste	144	106.90	26.05	3.23 **
Stress	Lower Caste	137	98.17	18.85	
Total Achievement	Upper Caste	144	212.03	50.86	3.11 **
Stress	Lower Caste	137	195.81	35.45	

*** Significant at 0.01 level*

Above Table reveals that the mean difference of upper caste and lower caste college girls on the frequency, quantity and total achievement stress differ significantly, when compared between the two means. The obtained t-values are 3.58, 3.23 and 3.11 respectively with 279 df. The difference regarding the frequency, quantity and total achievement stress is found to be statistically significant at 0.01 level of confidence. The upper caste college girls have more achievement stress than lower caste college girls. It was hypothesized that upper caste and lower caste college girls would differ significantly on their scores on the frequency, quantity and total achievement stress is totally accepted in the present study. The global view can be ascertained easily on the basis of graphical representation of data shown in Fig. 8.

The findings can be rationalized by their better family background and expectations regarding achievement from their family members and as well as society in case of upper caste students. However, in case of lower caste students, the social background of family set up generally does not motivate them to achieve something.

The outcome of analysis of upper caste and lower caste college girls on the frequency, quantity and total academic stress is available in Table- 4.18.

Table 4.18 Mean comparisons of upper caste and lower caste college girls on the frequency, quantity and total academic stress

Components	*Groups compared*	*N*	*Mean*	*SD*	*t*
Frequency of Academic	Upper Caste	144	155.87	30.54	3.45 **
Stress	Lower Caste	137	144.17	26.39	
Quantity of Academic	Upper Caste	144	154.50	30.19	2.67 **
Stress	Lower Caste	137	145.50	26.17	
Total Academic	Upper Caste	144	320.63	61.27	4.35 **
Stress	Lower Caste	137	291.83	49.47	

*** Significant at 0.01 level*

Table 4.18 presents comparisons of upper caste and lower caste college girls on the frequency, quantity and total academic stress. Means and standard deviations of the frequency, quantity and total academic stress for upper caste and lower caste college girls have been presented in the Table along with 't' values. The table reveals that the comparisons indicate significant difference between upper caste and lower caste college girls. The obtained t- values are 3.45, 2.67 and 4.35 respectively with 279 df. The two groups, however, statistically differ significantly at 0.01 level of confidence. The upper caste college girls have higher mean values than lower caste college girls. Thus, it is evident from the result that upper caste college girls have greater academic stress. The hypothesis formulated in this connection is therefore proved. A look into Fig. 8 confirms the above trends.

The finding can also be justified in terms of better academic level in the family and its expectations from the students regarding academic success.

A comparison of mean values of upper caste and lower caste college girls on the frequency, quantity and total physical stress has been reported in Table – 4.19.

Table 4.19 Mean comparisons of upper caste and lower caste college girls on the frequency, quantity and total physical stress

Components	*Groups compared*	*N*	*Mean*	*SD*	*t*
Frequency of Physical	Upper Caste	144	80.90	25.31	1.34 NS
Stress	Lower Caste	137	76.83	25.39	
Quantity of Physical	Upper Caste	144	80.17	28.29	1.25 NS
Stress	Lower Caste	137	84.31	27.56	
Total	upper caste	144	156.83	53.25	

(Contd.)

(Contd. Table 4.19)

Components	*Groups compared*	*N*	*Mean*	*SD*	*t*
Physical					1.27 NS
Stress	lower caste	137	164.76	50.77	

NS - Not significant

A comparison has been made in Table – 4.19 between upper caste and lower caste college girls on the frequency, quantity and total physical stress. The result gives a clear indication that none of the three comparisons show any significant difference between upper caste and lower caste college girls on this measure.

Although, there exists statistically insignificant difference between upper caste and lower caste college girls on the frequency, quantity and total physical stress. However it may be noted that upper caste college girls have slightly higher mean scores on the frequency of physical stress, but on the quantity and total physical stress, lower caste college girls obtained higher mean values than upper caste college girls. Thus the hypothesis formulated in this connection that upper caste and lower caste college girls would differ significantly on their scores on the frequency, quantity and total physical stress, is rejected in the present study. The result is further illustrated through the graph in Fig. 8.

Physical stress has been found to be almost of equal level perhaps because of the common role that the subject has to play in her routine life, i.e., of a typical Indian middle class girl contributing to her family work. But it is seen the physical stress score of upper caste students is lower than thoes of lower caste students. It may be because of the better socio-economic conditions, which leads to availability of various comforts and amenities.

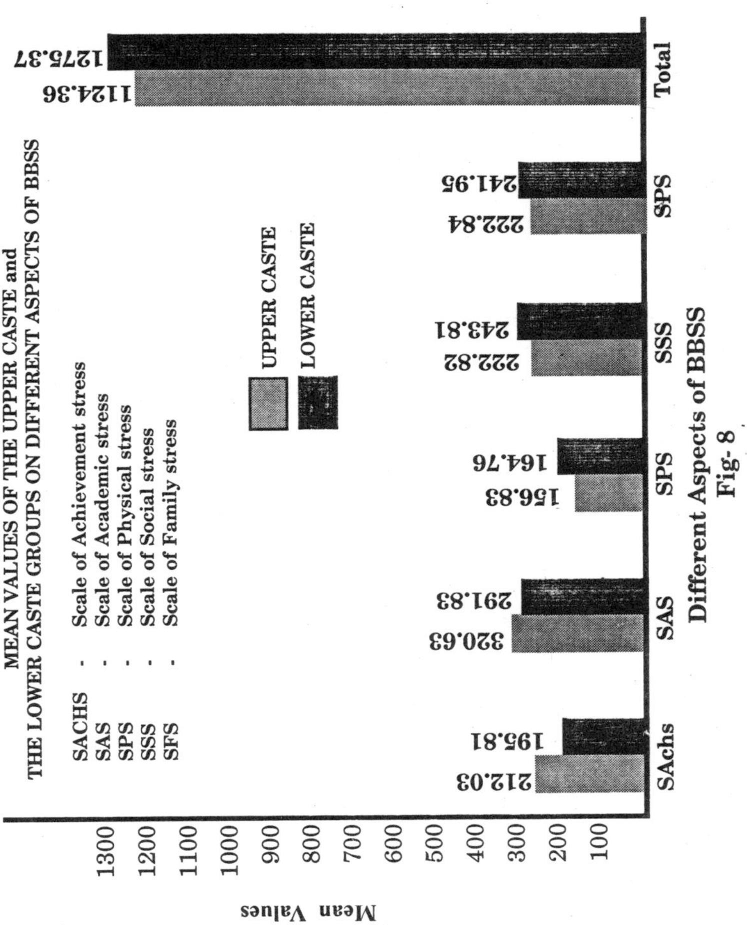
MEAN VALUES OF THE UPPER CASTE and
THE LOWER CASTE GROUPS ON DIFFERENT ASPECTS OF BBSS
SACHS - Scale of Achievement stress
SAS - Scale of Academic stress
SPS - Scale of Physical stress
SSS - Scale of Social stress
SFS - Scale of Family stress
UPPER CASTE
LOWER CASTE
Mean Values
1300
1200
1100
1000
900
800
700
600
500
400
300
200
100
212.03
195.81
320.63
291.83
156.83
164.76
222.82
243.81
222.84
241.95
1124.36
1275.37
SAchs
SAS
SPS
SSS
SPS
Total
Different Aspects of BBSS
Fig- 8

The outcome of analysis of upper caste and lower caste college girls on the frequency, quantity and total social stress is available in Table – 4.20.

Table 4.20 Mean comparisons of upper caste and lower caste college girls on the frequency, quantity and total social stress

Components	*Groups compared*	*N*	*Mean*	*SD*	*t*
Frequency of Social Stress	Upper Caste	144	109.17	24.18	2.97 **
	Lower Caste	137	120.60	36.79	
Quantity of Social Stress	Upper Caste	144	112.83	26.76	2.74 **
	Lower Caste	137	124.18	40.88	
Total Social Stress	Upper Caste	144	222.82	53.44	2.67 **
	Lower Caste	137	243.81	75.62	

*** Significant at 0.01 level*

The Table 4.20 presents comparisons of upper caste and lower caste college girls on the frequency, quantity and total social stress. A look into the Table reveals that the comparisons indicate significant difference between the mean scores of upper caste and lower caste college girls. The obtained t – values are 2.97, 2.74 and 2.67 respectively with 279 df. The two groups, however, differ significantly at 1% level of confidence. The lower caste college girls have higher mean values than upper caste college girls. Thus it is evident from the result that lower caste college girls have greater social stress. The hypothesis formulated in this connection is, therefore, proved. A look into the graph in Fig. 8 confirms the above trend.

The higher level of social stress among lower caste students can be attributed to various social constrains and reservations regarding caste related issues along with the inferior social status of the caste as a whole. Perhaps, because of the conservative conventions and norms of the society they want to get rid of it, because of which they are under higher social stress, whereas, in case of upper caste students, society is more liberal to allow them to change their role in the society.

A comparison of mean values of the upper caste and lower caste college girls on the frequency, quantity and total family stress has been reported in Table – 4.21.

Table - 4.21 Mean comparison of the upper caste and lower caste college girls on the frequency-quantity and total family stress

Components	*Groups compared*	*N*	*Mean*	*SD*	*t*
Frequency of Family Stress	Upper Caste	144	103.17	31.98	3.26 **
	Lower Caste	137	116.17	34.61	
Quantity of Family Stress	Upper Caste	144	115.83	36.67	2.00 *
	Lower Caste	137	124.77	37.89	
Total Family Stress	Upper Caste	144	222.84	65.56	2.32 *
	Lower Caste	137	241.95	71.79	

*** Significant at 0.01 level*

** Significant at 0.05 level*

Table 4.21 shows the comparison of mean scores of upper caste and lower caste college girls on the frequency quantity and total family stress. The mean values of the upper caste and lower caste college girls on the frequency-quantity and total family stress are 103.17, 116.17, 115.83, 124.77, 222.84 and 241.95 respectively with 31.98, 34.61, 36.67 , 37.89, 65.56 and 71.79 SDs. All the t-values as reflected in the Table (3.26, 2.00 and 2.32 with 279 df.) reveal that there is a significant difference between upper caste and lower caste college girls on the frequency quantity and total family stress. The lower caste college girls have higher mean values than upper caste college girls. Thus, it is evident from the result that lower caste college girls have more family stress. The hypothesis formulated in this connection is therefore proved. The tendency is well reflected in the graph as shown in Fig. 8.

Table 4.21 shows the comparison of mean scores of upper caste and lower caste college girls on the frequency, quantity and the total family stress. All the t-values as reflected in the Table (3.26, 2.00 and 2.32 with 279 df.) reveal that there is a significant difference between upper caste and lower caste college girls on the frequency, quantity and total family stress. The lower caste college girls have higher mean values than upper caste college girls. Thus, it is evident from the result that lower caste college girls have more family stress. The hypothesis formulated in this connection is therefore proved. The tendency is well reflected in the graph as shown in Fig. 8.

The finding can be again rationalized in the light of better educational and socio-economic conditions of upper caste college girls. Family stress has been found higher in case of lower caste students which can be attributed to lack of education, socio-economic conditions, lack of respectable outlook towards female and suppression of female in the family.

The outcome of analysis of upper caste and lower caste college girls on the frequency, quantity and total stress is available in Table – 4.22.

Table 4.22 Mean comparisons of upper caste and lower caste college girls on the frequency, quantity and total stress

Components	*Groups compared*	*N*	*Mean*	*SD*	*t*
Frequency of Total Stress	Upper Caste	144	557.75	138.09	5.00 **
	Lower Caste	137	640.00	137.15	
Quantity of Total Stress	Upper Caste	144	570.71	178.92	3.29 **
	Lower Caste	137	635.37	147.96	
Total Stress	Upper Caste	144	1124.36	317.01	4.19 **
	lower caste	137	1275.37	285.11	

*** Significant at 0.01 level*

In Table 4.22 a comparison between the upper caste and lower caste college girls is made on the scores obtained from frequency of total stress, quantity of total stress and grand total stress. The difference between the mean values in two groups *viz.*, upper caste and lower caste college girls has been found to be statistically significant. The obtained t-value are 5.00, 3.29 and 4.19 on frequency of total stress, quantity of total stress and grand total stress respectively. It may be noted that lower caste college girls have higher mean values than upper caste college girls. Thus, it is evident from the result that lower caste college girls are found to be more stressed than upper caste college girls. Thus, the hypothesis, formulated in this connection, is accepted in the present study. It was hypothesized that upper caste and lower caste college girls would differ significantly on their scores on the frequency of total stress, quantity of total stress and grand total stress. The total picture has been depicted very clearly in Fig. 8.

The total stress score of the lower caste college girls has been found to be higher than upper caste college girls because of the fact that they generally do not get respect in their family as well as society due to various social constraints and reservation regarding caste related issues. The members from their own society are not in a position to show respect towards them due to their conservative convention as well as inferior social status.

On the basis of findings of study of two groups *viz.*, upper caste and lower caste college girls on the various aspects of BBSS, following conclusions might be drawn.

1. The two groups in question *viz.*, upper caste and lower caste college girls did differ significantly on the frequency quantity and total achievement stress; frequency, quantity and total academic stress; frequency, quantity and total social stress; frequency, quantity and total family stress; frequency, quantity and total stress. The upper caste college girls obtained higher mean values on achievement and academic stress scale, but on social and family stress scale lower caste college girls, have higher mean value.

2. The two groups in question, however did not differ significantly on frequency, quantity and total physical stress.

Similar kind of analysis was done for the scores obtained on various aspects of BBSS by the three groups *viz.*, high, middle and low economic level college girls. The outcome of such analysis is available in Tables – 4.23 - 4.29.

Table 4.23 Mean scores of three groups *viz.*, high, middle and low economic level college girls on various types of stress on Bisht Battery of Stress Scale and as a whole

Groups	*SAchS*	*SAS*	*SPS*	*SSS*	*SFS*	*Total BBSS*
High	186.2	255.53	139.73	189.80	201.15	974.98
Middle	223.94	304.39	217.23	290.13	285.19	1300.75
Low	187.48	267.71	171.71	253.31	227.63	1080.98

The obtained data were subjected to analysis of variance (ANOVA) in accordance with the design of difference between the groups on various measures of stress. The 'F' ratio is the indicative of significance of difference among the groups considered for the present study.

The result of analysis of variance of frequency quantity and total achievement stress in relation to high, middle and low economic level college girls is available in Table - 4.24.

Table 4.24 Summary of analysis of variance in respect to high, middle and low economic level college girls on the frequency quantity and total achievement stress.

Components	*Groups compared*	*N*	*Mean*	*SD*	*F*
Frequency of	Between group	2	445.28	222.64	
Achievement					3.44 *
Stress	Within group	27	1742.42	64.54	
Quantity of	Between group	2	314.48	175.24	
Achievement					1.88 NS
Stress	Within group	27	2334.10	83.36	
Total	Between group	2	544.24	272.14	
Achievement					4.058 *
Stress	Within group	27	1676.43	67.05	

** Significant at 0.05 level*
NS Not significant

Table 4.24 presents summary of analysis of variance (ANOVA) of the frequency, quantity and total achievement stress. The obtained values of 'F' ratio for three groups *viz.*, high, middle and low economic level college girls turned to be significant at 0.01 level of confidence on frequency of achievement stress and total achievement stress (F= 3.44 df 2/27 and 4.058 df = 2/25). The three groups do not differ significantly on quantity of achievement stress (F= 1.88 df = 2/28). Thus the hypothesis formulated in this connection is partially accepted. The graph in Fig. 9 clearly depicts the trend.

The finding can be rationalized due to the fact that students of middle economic level wanted to achieve more but they are not in a position to get economic support from their family.

Summary of analysis of variance in respect of high, middle and low economic level college girls on the frequency quantity and total academic stress is available in Table – 4.25.

Table 4.25 Summary of analysis of variance in respect to high, middle and low economic level college girls on the frequency quantity and total academic stress

Components	*Groups compared*	*N*	*Mean*	*SD*	*F*
Frequency of Academic Stress	Between group	2	219.25	109.63	0.761 NS
	Within group	21	3022.75	143.94	
Quantity of Academic Stress	Between group	2	303.13	151.56	1.26 NS
	Within group	22	2636.87	119.85	
Total Academic Stress	Between group	2	242.48	121.24	1.029 NS
	Within group	22	2589.95	117.72	

NS Not significant

In Table 4.25 a comparison has been made between high, middle and low economic level college girls on the frequency quantity and total academic stress. The Table reveals that none of the three comparisons namely, frequency of academic stress, quantity of academic stress and total academic stress shows any significant difference between high, middle and low economic level college girls. Although no significant difference between the high, middle and low economic level college girls has been reported in this comparison, but the trend indicates that the middle economic level college girls have greater mean score on total academic stress. The hypothesis formulated in this connection that the high, middle and low economic level college girls would differ significantly on their scores on the frequency, quantity and total academic stress, is rejected in the present study. Fig. 9 clearly depicts the trend.

The results of analysis of variance of the frequency-quantity and total physical stress in relation to high, middle and low economic level college girls is available in Table 4.26.

Table 4.26 Summary of analysis of variance in respect to high, middle and low economic level college girls on the frequency quantity and total physical stress

Components	*Groups compared*	*N*	*Mean*	*SD*	*F*
Frequency of Physical Stress	Between group	2	167.55	83.77	1.273 NS
	Within group	27	1776.45	65.79	
Quantity of Physical Stress	Between group	2	44.32	72.16	0.408 NS
	Within group	27	4773.68	176.80	
Total Physical Stress	Between group	2	123.23	61.61	0.861 NS
	Within group	28	2003.55	71.55	

NS Not significant

The summary of ANOVA of the frequency, quantity and total physical stress is presented in Table 4.26 and results indicate that none of the three comparisons namely, frequency of physical stress, quantity of physical stress and total physical stress have shown any significant difference between the high, middle and low economic level college girls. It may be noted that no effect is found in case of economic level. Although there is no statistically significant difference between the high, middle and low economic level college girls, but it may be noted that the middle economic level college girls have greater mean value on the total physical stress. Thus the hypothesis formulated in this connection is rejected in the present study. The result is further illustrated in Fig. 9.

The results of analysis of variance of the frequency quantity and total social stress in relation to high, middle and low economic level college girls would be available in Table 4.27.

Table 4.27 Summary of analysis of variance in respect to high, middle and low economic level college girls on the frequency, quantity and total social stress

Components	*Groups compared*	*N*	*Mean*	*SD*	*F*
Frequency of Social Stress	Between group	2	328.59	164.29	1.29 NS
	Within group	26	3297.97	126.84	
Quantity of Social Stress	Between group	2	304.51	152.29	1.79 NS
	Within group	24	2040.10	85.00	
Total Social Stress	Between group	2	370.72	185.36	2.175 NS
	Within group	25	2133.00	85.32	

NS Not significant.

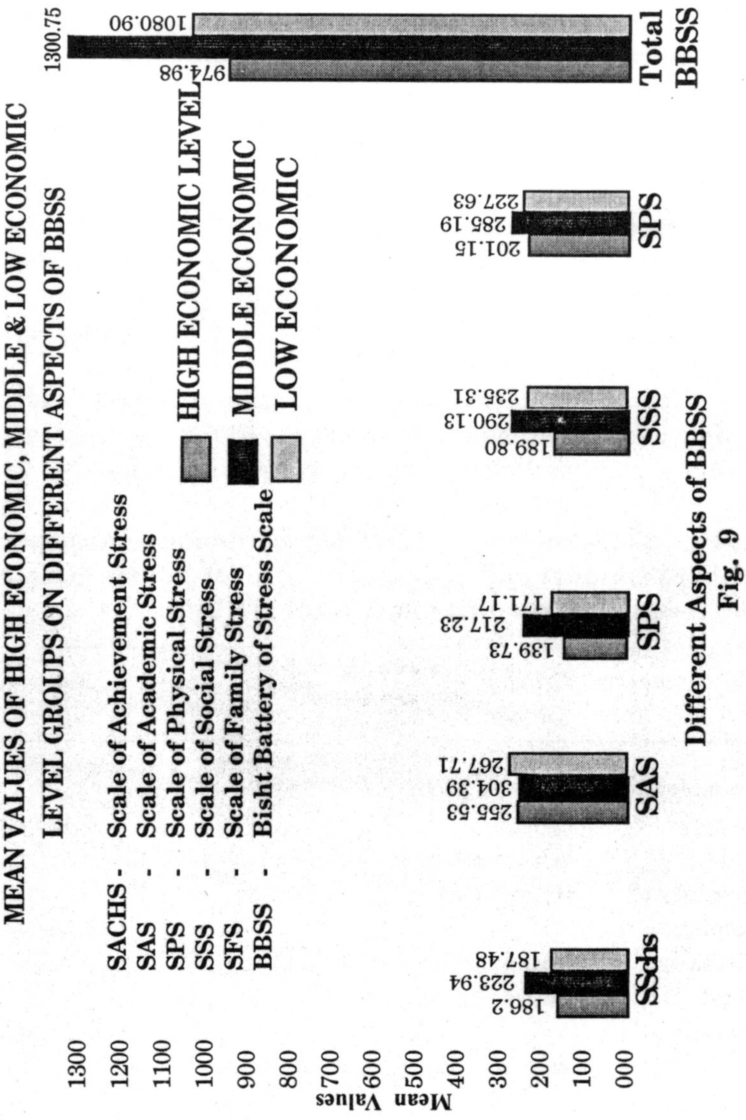
MEAN VALUES OF HIGH ECONOMIC, MIDDLE & LOW ECONOMIC LEVEL GROUPS ON DIFFERENT ASPECTS OF BBSS
SACHS - Scale of Achievement Stress
SAS - Scale of Academic Stress
SPS - Scale of Physical Stress
SSS - Scale of Social Stress
SFS - Scale of Family Stress
BBSS - Bisht Battery of Stress Scale
HIGH ECONOMIC LEVEL
MIDDLE ECONOMIC
LOW ECONOMIC
Mean Values
1300
1200
1100
1000
900
800
700
600
500
400
300
200
100
000
186.2
223.94
187.48
255.53
304.39
267.71
139.73
217.23
171.17
189.80
290.13
235.31
201.15
285.19
227.63
974.98
1300.75
1080.90
SSchs
SAS
SPS
SSS
SPS
Total BBSS
Different Aspects of BBSS
Fig. 9

A look into the Table 4.27 reveals summary of ANOVA of the frequency, quantity and total social stress. The following main points may be observed in this Table that economic levels have no effect on the frequency, quantity and total social stress. It is indicated that there is no significant difference between high, middle and low economic level college girls on the frequency, quantity and total social stress. Thus, the hypothesis formulated in this connection that high, middle and low economic level college girls would differ significantly on their scores on the frequency, quantity and total social stress, is rejected. But if we see the mean values of three groups, it may be noted that the middle economic level college girls obtained highest mean values on the total social stress. Fig. 9 clearly depicts the trend.

The summary of analysis of variance in respect to high, middle and low economic level college girls on the frequency-quantity and total family stress is presented in Table – 4.28.

Table 4.28 Summary of analysis of variance in respect to high, middle and low economic level college girls on the frequency, quantity and total family stress

Components	*Groups compared*	*N*	*Mean*	*SD*	*F*
Frequency of Family Stress	Between group	2	141.69	70.85	0.428 NS
	Within group	22	3634.31	165.19	
Quantity of Family Stress	Between group	2	294.25	147.13	1.167 NS
	Within group	23	2092.22	90.96	
Total Family Stress	Between group	2	242.49	121.25	1.18 NS
	Within group	23	2361.18	102.6	

NS Not significant

Table 4.28 presents summary of ANOVA of the frequency, quantity and total family stress. The Table reveals that none of the three comparisons namely, frequency, quantity and total family stress have shown any significant difference between the high, middle and low economic level college girls. Although, there is no significant difference between the three groups *viz.*, high, middle and low economic level college girls, but it may be noted that the middle economic level college girls have highest mean scores on the total family stress. Thus, the hypothesis formulated in this connection that high, middle and low economic level college girls would differ significantly on their scores on the frequency-quantity and total family stress, is rejected in the present study. The graph in Fig. 9 clearly depicts the trend.

The result of analysis of variance of the frequency, quantity and total stress in relations to the high, middle and low economic level college girls is available in Table – 4.29.

Table 4.29 Summary of analysis of variance in respect to high, middle and low economic level college girls on the frequency- quantity and total stress

Components	*Groups compared*	*N*	*Mean*	*SD*	*t*
Frequency of Total Stress	Between group	2	226.35	113.18	0.990 NS
	Within group	25	2855.36	114.21	
Quantity of Total Stress	Between group	2	170.66	85.33	1.11 NS
	Within group	29	2226.83	76.78	
Total Stress	Between group	2	142.32	72.16	0.740 NS
	Within group	27	2611.68	96.72	

NS Not significant

The summary of ANOVA of the frequency, quantity and the total stress is presented in Table – 4.29. The results indicate that none of the three comparisons namely, frequency of total stress, quantity of total stress and total stress have shown any significant difference between high, middle and low economic level college girls. It may be noted that no effect is found in case of economic level. Although there is no statistically significant difference between high, middle and low economic level college girls, it may be noted that the middle economic level college girls obtained highest mean values on the total stress. Thus the hypothesis formulated in this connection is rejected in the present study. The global view can be ascertained easily on the basis of graphical representation of data in Fig. 9.

Although there is no statistically significant difference between the high, middle and low economic level college girls, but it may be noted that the middle economic level college girls, have the highest mean values on all type of stress score as well as grand total stress score.

The findings can be rationalized in this context as college girls of low economic status have no other option except either to live with it or to raise it. Similarly the students of high economic status have limited options – either to maintain the existing or to lower down it. But for the students, belonging to middle economic stratum, there is always dilemma and ambiguity so as to maintain the *status quo* or to move up or to go down. The above ambiguity often leads to so much of anxiety, that in due course of time it results in various types of stress.

Fig. 10 presents a graphic representation of arts and science, high, middle and low economic level groups in various combinations.

Fig. 11 would provide a quick glance of outcome as a whole.

On the basis of findings of study of the three groups *viz.*, high, middle and low economic level college girls on various aspects of BBSS, following conclusions might be drawn :

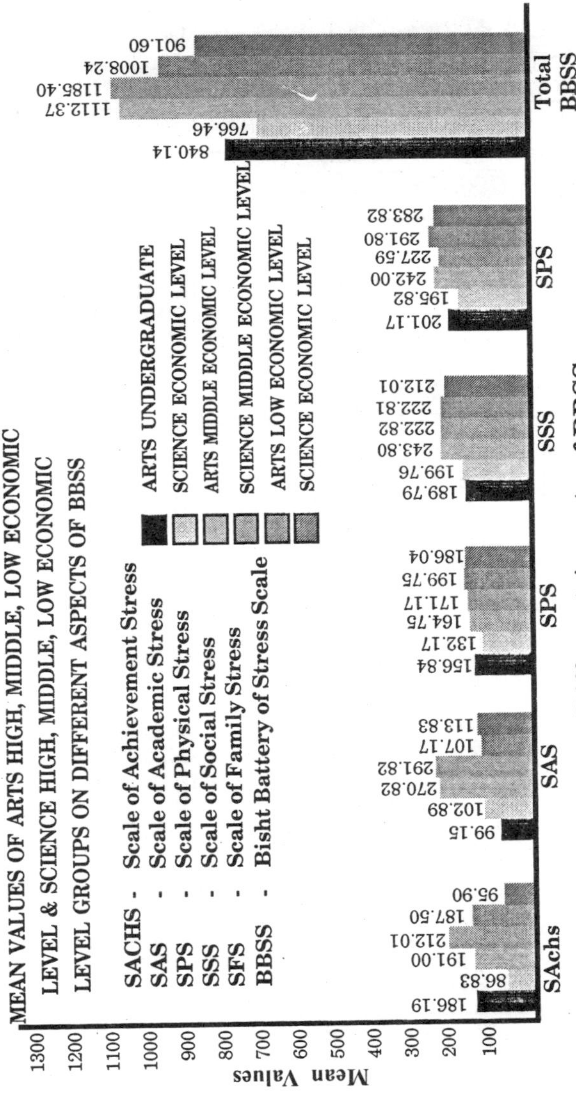

Different Aspects of BBSS
Fig. - 10

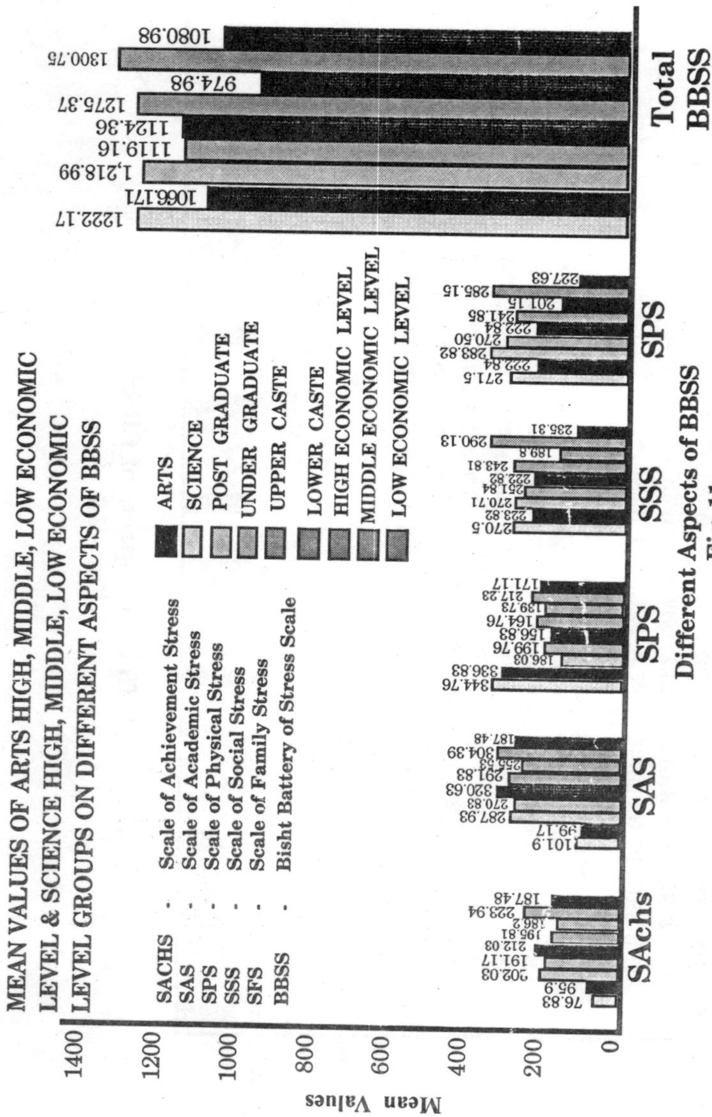
MEAN VALUES OF ARTS HIGH, MIDDLE, LOW ECONOMIC LEVEL & SCIENCE HIGH, MIDDLE, LOW ECONOMIC LEVEL GROUPS ON DIFFERENT ASPECTS OF BBSS
SACHS . Scale of Achievement Stress
SAS . Scale of Academic Stress
SPS . Scale of Physical Stress
SSS . Scale of Social Stress
SFS . Scale of Family Stress
BBSS . Bisht Battery of Stress Scale
ARTS
SCIENCE
POST GRADUATE
UNDER GRADUATE
UPPER CASTE
LOWER CASTE
HIGH ECONOMIC LEVEL
MIDDLE ECONOMIC LEVEL
LOW ECONOMIC LEVEL
Mean Values
SAchs
SAS
SPS
SSS
SPS
Total BBSS
Different Aspects of BBSS
Fig. 11

1. The three groups in question *viz.*, high, middle and low economic level of college girls did differ significantly only on the frequency of achievement stress and total achievement stress.
2. The three groups in question, however, did not differ significantly on the quantity of achievement stress, frequency, quantity and total academic stress; frequency, quantity and physical stress; frequency, quantity, and social stress; frequency, quantity and family stress, and frequency of total stress, quantity of total stress, and grand total stress.

Similar kind of analysis was done for the scores obtained on various aspects of Middlesex Hospital Questionnaire by the subjects. The outcome of such analysis is available in Tables 4.30 to 4.34.

The data obtained on different independent variables *viz.*, curriculum, level of education, caste and economic level on the MHQ were analyzed adapting t-test and F-test of significance. The curriculum had two groups – arts and science. Level of education had two groups, post graduate and under graduate. Caste had also two groups – upper caste and lower caste. Economic level had three groups – high, middle and low. The t-test of significance was used where there were only two groups and ANOVA was used where there were more than two groups. The dependent variable, neurotic behaviour, had six sub-areas and one total score. This way, analysis was done on seven dependent variable scores. The measurement was done with the help of Middlesex Hospital Questionnaire.

The outcome of analysis of arts and science students on MHQ and its different aspects is available in Table – 4.30.

A comparison has been made in Table 4.30 between arts and science groups on MHQ and its different aspects. Means and standard deviations of MHQ and its different aspects for arts and science groups have been presented in the Table along

Table - 4.30 Mean comparison of arts and science students on MHQ and its various aspects

Aspects of MHQ	*Groups compared*	*N*	*Mean*	*SD*	*t-Value*
FFA	Arts	150	6.52	3.44	3.80**
	Science	150	5.32	2.36	
OBS	Arts	150	7.76	2.61	2.45*
	Science	150	7.00	2.85	
PHO	Arts	150	5.98	2.84	2.66**
	Science	150	5.15	2.57	
SOM	Arts	150	4.38	2.71	1.10NS
	Science	150	4.05	2.48	
DEP	Arts	150	5.70	2.61	6.30 NS
	Science	150	5.90	2.83	
HYS	Arts	150	5.39	2.41	2.23**
	Science	150	4.73	2.50	
Total MHQ	Arts	150	36.44	11.18	3.38 **
	Science	150	32.60	8.26	

*** Significant at 0.01 level*
** Significant at 0.05 level*
NS Not Significant

with 't values. The result gives a clear indication that the four aspects *viz.*, FFA, OBS, PHO, HYS and the total MHQ, show significant difference between arts and science groups. The arts group obtained higher mean values than thoes of the science group. The two groups differ significantly on their scores on FFA with regards to the mean values 6.52 and 5.32; on PHO with 2.84 and 2.57 mean values; on total MHQ with 36.44 and 32.60 mean values respectively. The t-ratio 3.80, 2.66 and 3.38 is found to be significant at 0.01 level of confidence. The two groups differ significantly on their scores on OBS and HYS with mean values of 7.76 and 7.00; 5.39 and 4.73 respectively with 't' ratio 2.45 and 2.23. Which is found to be significant at 0.05 level of confidence. This clearly indicates that arts group has more neurotic behaviour than science group. No significant mean difference has been found in this group on the measures of SOM and DEP. This indicates that the difference observed on mean values had come due to chance factor on these two aspects. The hypothesis formed in this connection that the groups with curriculum arts may differ significantly on their scores on MHQ and its different aspects than the group with curriculum science is, therefore, partially accepted. The result is further illustrated in Fig. 12.

The arts students had higher degree of free floating anxiety, perhaps due to uncertainties of future employment in the Indian setting. The science group, on the other hand, have a bright future of employment. The arts students had higher mean values on hysterical traits perhaps, due to their imaginative course structure. Science students need systematic and hard studies; hence, possibility of hysteric traits would be less in them.

On the basis of finding of study of the two groups *viz.*, arts and science college girls on the various aspects of MHQ, the following conclusions might be drawn:

1. The two groups in question *viz.*, arts and science, did differ significantly on free floating anxiety, obsessive

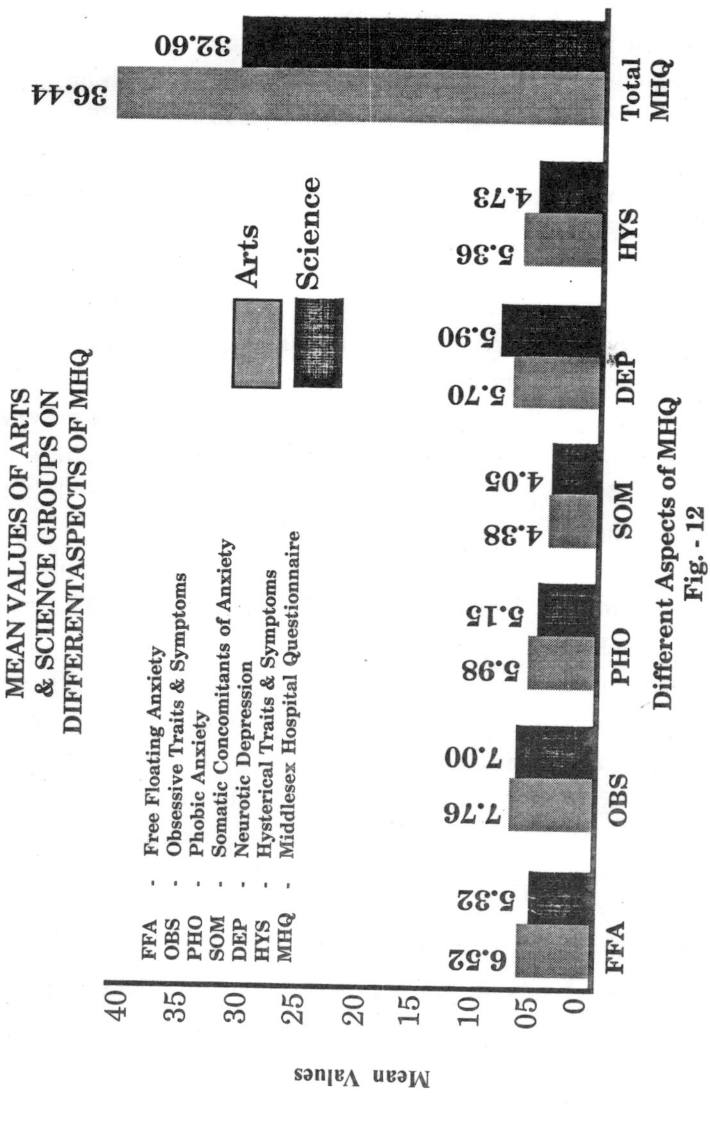
MEAN VALUES OF ARTS
& SCIENCE GROUPS ON
DIFFERENTASPECTS OF MHQ
FFA : Free Floating Anxiety
OBS : Obsessive Traits & Symptoms
PHO : Phobic Anxiety
SOM : Somatic Concomitants of Anxiety
DEP : Neurotic Depression
HYS : Hysterical Traits & Symptoms
MHQ : Middlesex Hospital Questionnaire
Arts
Science
Mean Values
40
35
30
25
20
15
10
05
0
6.52
5.32
7.76
7.00
5.98
5.15
4.38
4.05
5.70
5.90
5.36
4.73
36.44
32.60
FFA
OBS
PHO
SOM
DEP
HYS
Total MHQ
Different Aspects of MHQ
Fig. - 12

traits and symptoms, phobic anxiety, hysterical traits and total MHQ scores. The arts students have higher mean values than those of science students.

2. The two groups, in question, however, did not differ significantly on the two aspects *viz.*, somatic concomitants of anxiety and neurotic depression.

Similar kind of analysis was done for the scores obtained on various aspects of MHQ by the two groups *viz.*, under graduate and post graduate college girls. The outcome of such analysis is available in Table 4.31.

The outcome of analysis of post graduate and under graduate students on MHQ and its different aspects is given in Table 4.31.

In Table 4.31 a comparison between post graduate and under graduate college girls is made on the scores obtained from Middlesex Hospital Questionnaire and its sub-tests. The difference between the mean values in two groups has been found to be insignificant (t = 0.967 and t= 0.937 respectively) on OBS and PHO. But it may be noted that the post graduate college girls have higher mean scores than under graduate college girls. The two groups, however, differ significantly (t= 4.09, 2.96,3.69, 3.21, 3.58 respectively) on the measures of FFA, SOM, DEP, HYS and Total MHQ. Thus, it is evident from the result that post graduate college girls have more neurotic behaviour than under graduate college girls. The hypothesis formulated in this connection is partially accepted. A look into Fig. 13 confirms the above trends.

The post graduate students had higher degree of free floating anxiety, neurotic depression than under graduate students, perhaps due to uncertainty of employment and more anxiety for their career than under graduate students. Post graduate students are expected to face the problems of employment immediately as compared to the under graduate students.

Table 4.31 Mean comparisons of post graduate and under graduate students on MHQ and its different aspects

Aspects of MHQ	*Groups compared*	*N*	*Mean*	*SD*	*t-Value*
FFA	Post Graduate	150	6.82	3.04	4.09 **
	Under Graduate	150	5.46	2.73	
OBS	Post Graduate	150	8.18	2.86	0.967 NS
	Under Graduate	150	7.88	2.63	
PHO	Post Graduate	150	6.14	2.91	0.937 NS
	Under Graduate	150	5.84	2.66	
SOM	Post Graduate	150	4.80	2.77	2.96 **
	Under Graduate	150	3.94	2.33	
DEP	Post Graduate	150	6.58	3.03	3.69 **
	Under Graduate	150	5.36	2.68	
HYS	Post Graduate	150	5.74	2.71	3.21 **
	Under Graduate	150	4.84	2.19	
Total MHQ	Post Graduate	150	37.60	11.08	3.58 **
	Under Graduate	150	33.50	8.54	

*** Significant at 0.01 level*
NS Not Significant

Fig. 14 presents a graphical representation of arts, science, under graduate and post graduate groups in various combinations.

On the basis of findings of study on the two groups *viz.*, Post graduate and under graduate college girls on the various aspects of MHQ, the following conclusions might be drawn :

MEAN VALUES OF POST GRADUATE AND UNDERGRADUATE GROUPS ON DIFFERENT ASPECTS OF MHQ

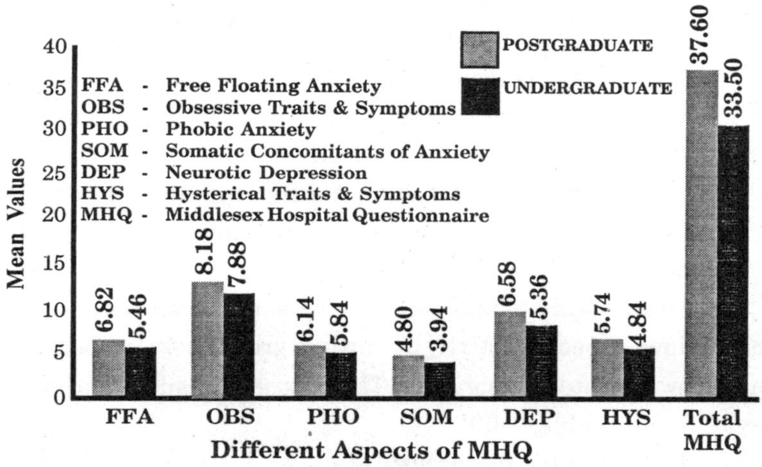

Fig. 13

MEAN VALUES OF ARTS UNDERGRADUATE, SCIENCE UNDER GRADUATE AND ARTS POST GRADUATE, SCIENCE POST GRADUATE GROUPS ON DIFFERENT ASPECTS OF MHQ.

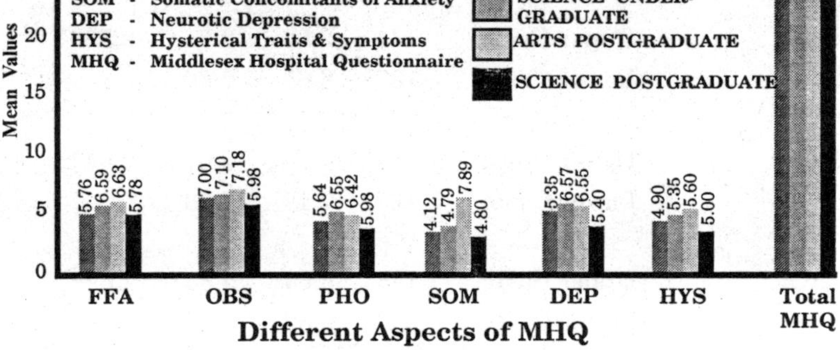

Fig. 14

1. The two groups in question *viz.*, post graduate and under graduate college girls did differ significantly on free floating anxiety, somatic commitments of anxiety, neurotic depression, hysterical traits and symptoms and total MHQ scores. Post graduate students obtained higher mean values than of the under graduate students.
2. The two groups *viz.*, post graduate and under graduate college girls however did not differ significantly on two aspects *viz.*, obsessive traits and symptoms and phobic anxiety.

Similar kind of analysis was done for the scores obtained on various aspects of MHQ by the two groups *viz.*, upper caste and lower caste college girls. The outcome of such analysis is available in Table - 4.32.

The outcome of analysis of upper caste and lower caste female students on MHQ and its different aspects is presented in Table – 4.32.

Table 4.32 Mean comparisons of upper caste and lower caste college girls on MHQ and its various aspects

Aspects of MHQ	*Groups compared*	*N*	*Mean*	*SD*	*t-value*
FFA	Upper Caste	144	5.80	2.91	2.50**
	Lower Caste	137	6.65	2.86	
OBS	Upper Caste	144	4.78	2.67	7.44**
	Lower Caste	137	7.17	2.73	
PHO	Upper Caste	144	5.64	2.64	2.69**
	Lower Caste	137	6.53	3.07	

(Contd.)

(Contd.Table 4.32)

Aspects of MHQ	*Groups compared*	*N*	*Mean*	*SD*	*t-value*
SOM	Upper Caste	144	4.11	2.89	
					11.48**
	Lower Caste	137	7.91	2.66	
DEP	Upper Caste	144	5.39	2.47	
					3.43**
	Lower Caste	137	6.53	3.07	
HYS	Upper Caste	144	4.99	2.38	
					2.35*
	Lower Caste	137	5.59	1.40	
Total MHQ	Upper Caste	144	32.73	9.84	
					4.56**
Lower Caste	137	38.25	10.56		

*** Significant at 0.01 level*
** Significant at 0.05 level*

A glance at Table 4.32 would reveal that the two groups *viz.*, upper caste and lower caste did differ significantly on MHQ and its various aspects *viz.*, FFA, OBS, PHO, SOM, DEP and HYS. The obtained values on FFA, OBS, PHO, SOM, DEP, HYS and total MHQ are 2.50, 7.44, 2.69, 11.48, 3.43, 2.35 and 4.56 respectively. Which is found to be significant at 0.01 and 0.05 level of probability. This clearly indicates and confirms the hypothesis that the so called lower caste college girls have more neurotic behaviour than that of so called upper caste college girls. Thus, the hypothesis is proved. The result is illustrated by the graph in Fig. 15.

The findings can be rationalized by their better family background and expectations regarding achievement from their family members and the society as well as in case of the upper

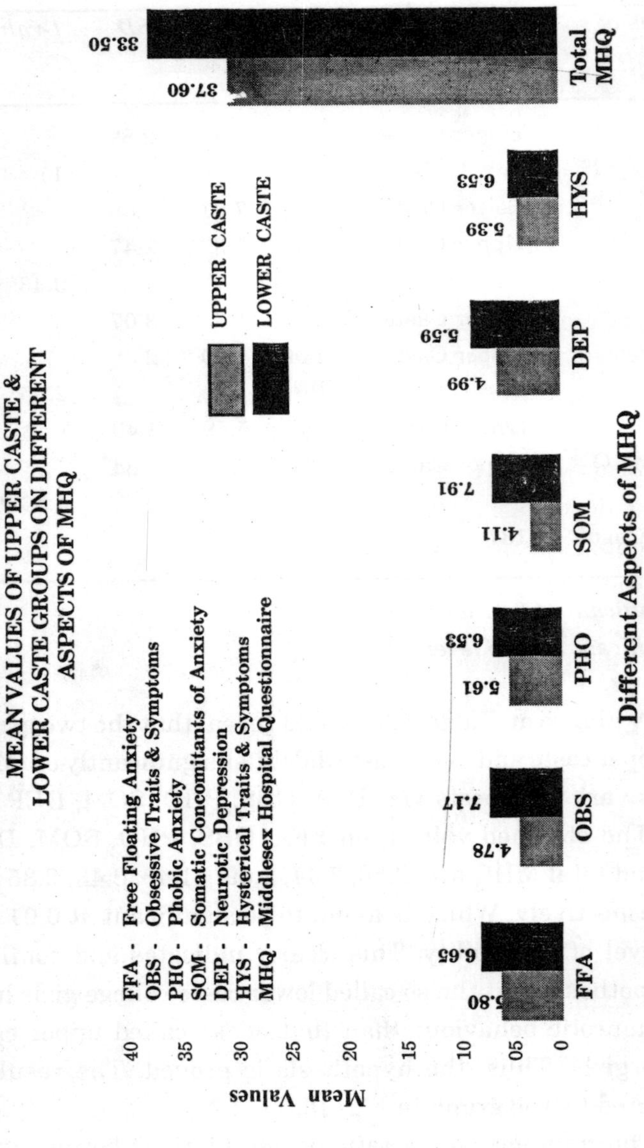
MEAN VALUES OF UPPER CASTE & LOWER CASTE GROUPS ON DIFFERENT ASPECTS OF MHQ
FFA - Free Floating Anxiety
OBS - Obsessive Traits & Symptoms
PHO - Phobic Anxiety
SOM - Somatic Concomitants of Anxiety
DEP - Neurotic Depression
HYS - Hysterical Traits & Symptoms
MHQ - Middlesex Hospital Questionnaire
UPPER CASTE
LOWER CASTE
Mean Values
40
35
30
25
20
15
10
05
0
5.80
6.65
4.78
7.17
5.61
6.53
4.11
7.91
4.99
5.59
5.39
6.53
37.60
33.50
FFA
OBS
PHO
SOM
DEP
HYS
Total MHQ
Different Aspects of MHQ

Fig- 15

caste college girls. However, in case of lower caste college girls, the social background of the family setup does not generally motivate them to achieve something.

On the basis of findings of study on the two groups *viz.*, upper and lower caste college girls on various aspects MHQ, the following conclusions might be drawn.

The two groups in question *viz.*, upper caste and lower caste college girls did differ significantly on free floating anxiety, obsessive traits and symptoms, phobic anxiety, hysterical traits and symptoms, somatic commitments of anxiety, neurotic depression and total MHQ scores. The lower caste students have higher mean values than thoes of the upper caste students.

Analysis of Variance was done for the scores obtained on various aspects of MHQ by the three groups *viz.*, high economic level, middle economic level and low economic level students. The outcome of such analysis is available in Table 4.33 and 4.34.

Table 4.33 Mean scores of three groups *viz.*, high, middle and low economic level college girls on various aspects of MHQ and on total MHQ scores.

Groups	*FFA*	*OBS*	*PHO*	*SOM*	*DEP*	*HYS*	*Total MHQ*
High	7.39	7.33	5.23	3.89	4.67	4.62	31.52
Middle	7.41	8.57	6.47	5.37	7.03	5.89	32.59
Low	4.96	7.21	5.94	3.29	4.83	4.82	31.41

The obtained data were subjected to analysis of variance (ANOVA) in accordance with the design of the difference between the groups on the various aspects of neurotic behaviour. The 'p' ratio is indicative of the significance of

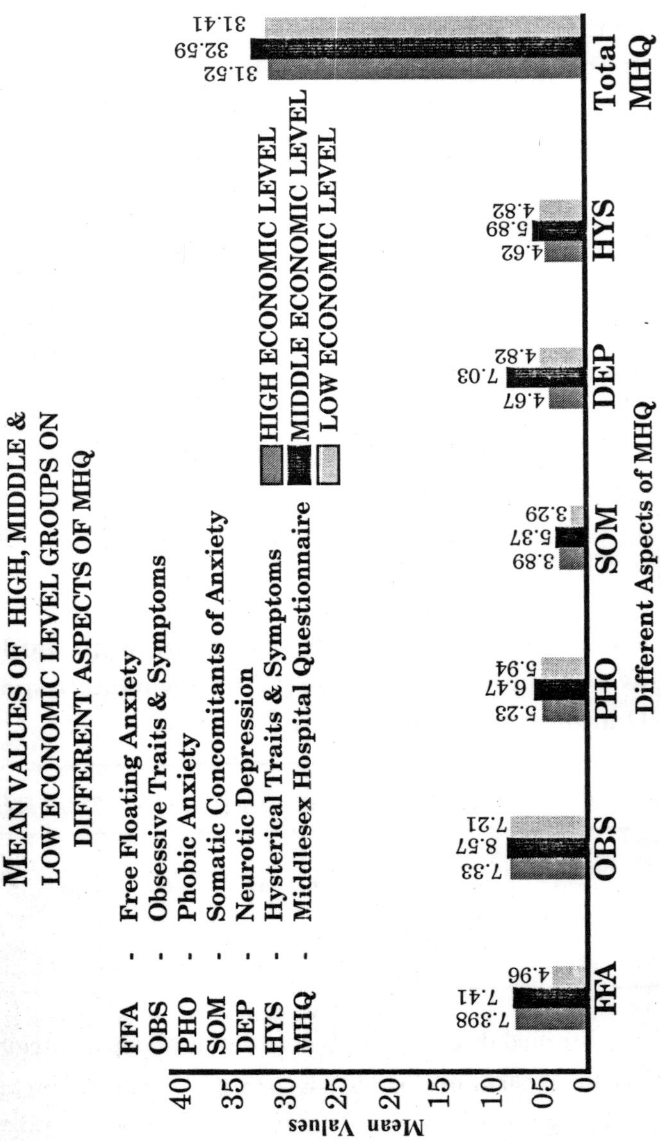
MEAN VALUES OF HIGH, MIDDLE & LOW ECONOMIC LEVEL GROUPS ON DIFFERENT ASPECTS OF MHQ
FFA . Free Floating Anxiety
OBS . Obsessive Traits & Symptoms
PHO . Phobic Anxiety
SOM . Somatic Concomitants of Anxiety
DEP . Neurotic Depression
HYS . Hysterical Traits & Symptoms
MHQ . Middlesex Hospital Questionnaire
HIGH ECONOMIC LEVEL
MIDDLE ECONOMIC LEVEL
LOW ECONOMIC LEVEL
Mean Values
40
35
30
25
20
15
10
05
0
7.398
7.41
4.96
7.33
8.57
7.21
5.23
6.47
5.94
3.89
5.37
3.29
4.67
7.03
4.82
4.62
5.89
4.82
31.52
32.59
31.41
FFA
OBS
PHO
SOM
DEP
HYS
Total MHQ
Different Aspects of MHQ

Fig. 16

difference among the groups and isconsidered for the present research.

Summary of analysis of variance in respect of high, middle and low economic level students on MHQ and its various aspects is given in Table – 4.34.

It is evident from the Table 4.34 that the obtained values of 'F' ratio for high, middle and low economic level college girls on MHQ and its various sub-tests; only FFA and HYS have significant difference (F =5.36, df. 2/12, P < .01 and F = 4.302, df 2/12, P < .01 respectively). Although, statistically the higher, middle and low economic level college girls do not differ significantly on OBS, PHO, SOM, DEP and Total MHQ scores, but it may be noted that the middle economic level college girls have obtained highest mean scores on the various aspects of MHQ and also as a whole. Hence, the hypothesis formulated in this regard is partially proved. The trend is very clearly depicted in the graph Fig. 16.

Table - 4.34 Summary of analysis of variance in respect of high, middle and low economic level college girls on MHQ and its various aspects

Different Aspects of MHQ	*Source*	*SS*	*MS*	*df*	*F*
FFA	Between group	350	175	2	5.36*
	Within group	776	35.5	12	
OBS	Between group	438.5	219.25	2	0.554 NS
	Within group	4261.5	473.5	9	

(Contd.Table 4.34)

(Contd.Table 4.34)

Different Aspects of MHQ	*Source*	*SS*	*MS*	*df*	*F*
PHO	Between group	350	175	2	0.738 NS
	Within group	2844	237	12	
SOM	Between group	452.68	226.34	2	0.631 NS
	Within group	3940.75	538.25	11	
DEP	Between group	196.23	18.13	2	0.384 NS
	Within group	253.7	225.47	10	
HYS	Between group	350	175	2	4.302*
	Within group	488	406.7	12	
Total MHQ	Between group	141.69	70.85	2	0.845 NS
	Within group	1844.30	83.82	22	

** Significant at 0.05 level.*

NS Not significant

The findings can be rationalized in this context that the college girls of high economic stratum, have no more option except either to live with it or to raise it. Similarity, the students of low economic stratum have limited options – either to maintain the existing level or to lower down it. But for the students, belonging to the middle economic stratum, there is always dilemma and ambiguity so as to maintain the *status quo* or to move up or to go down. The above ambiguity often leads to such an anxiety, which in due course, results in various types of stress, which is reflected in neurotic behaviour.

MEAN VALUES OF ARTS (HIGH, MIDDLE LOW ECONOMIC LEVEL) AND SCIENCE (HIGH, MIDDLE, LOW ECONOMIC LEVEL) GROUPS ON DIFFERENT ASPECTS OF MHQ

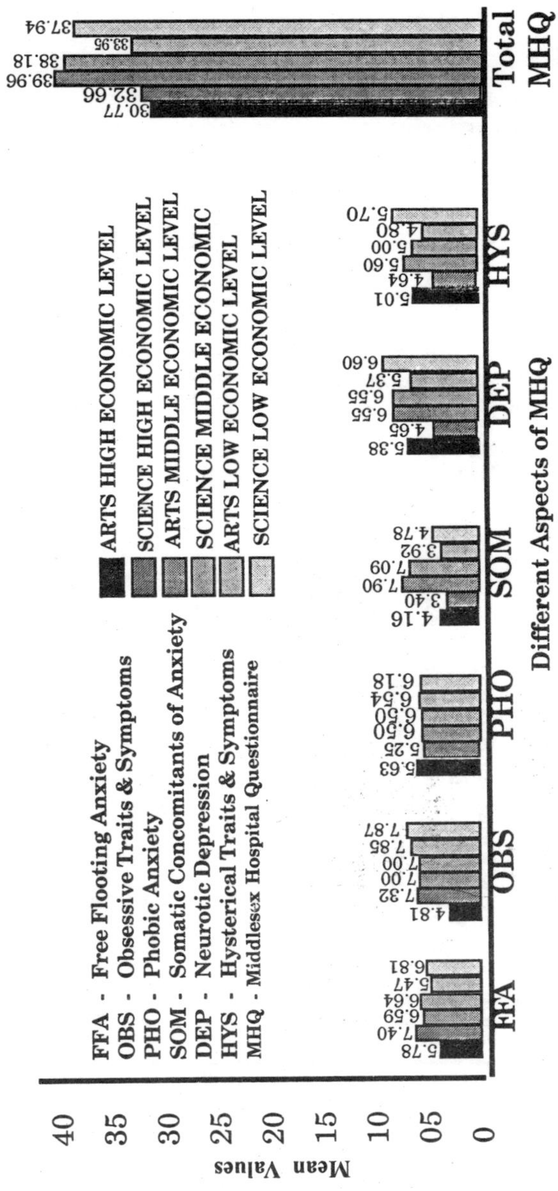

Different Aspects of MHQ

Fi.g. 17

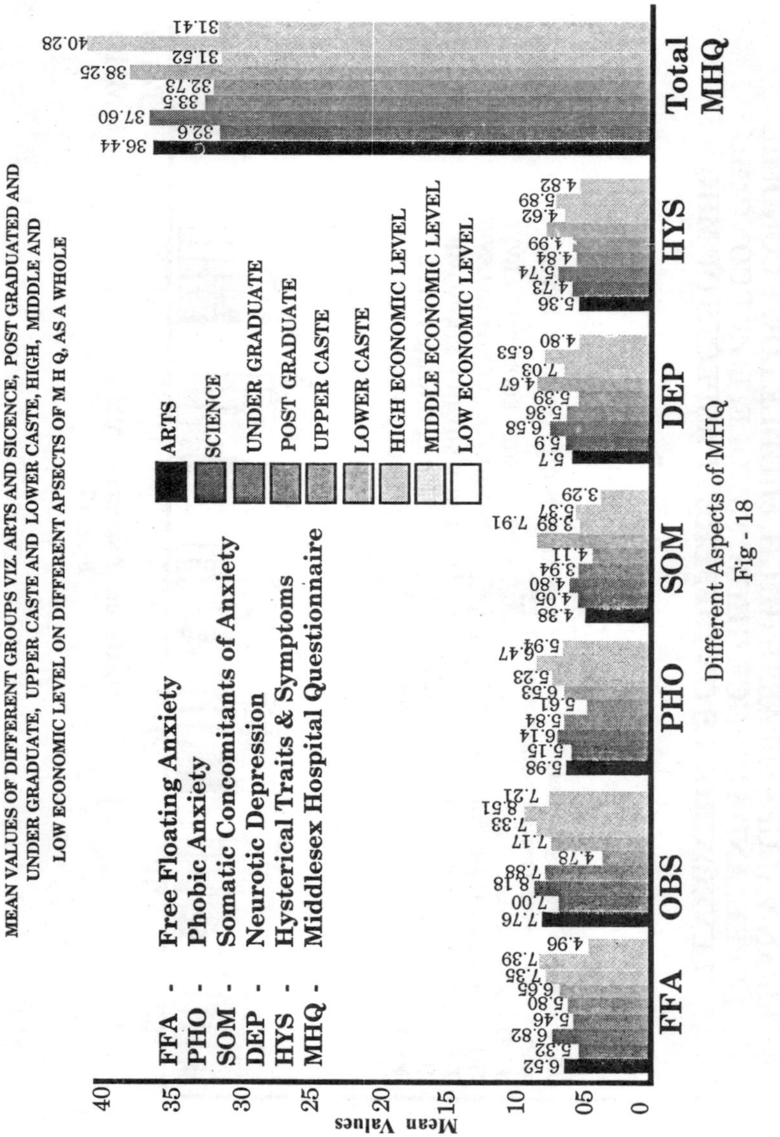

Different Aspects of MHQ

Fig - 18

Fig. 17 presents a graphic representation of arts and science (high, middle and low economic level) groups in various combinations.

Fig. 18 provides a quick glace of outcome as a whole.

On the basis of findings of study of the three groups *viz.*, high, middle and low economic level college girls on the various aspects of MHQ, the following conclusions might be drawn :

1. The three groups in question *viz.*, high, middle and low economic level college girls did differ significantly on the free floating anxiety and hysterical traits and symptoms.
2. The three groups in questions, however, did not differ significantly on obsessive traits and symptoms, phobic anxiety, somatic concomitants of anxiety, neurotic depressions as well as total MHQ scores.

General Conclusions

On the basis of findings of study the following general conclusions were drawn :

1. The hypothesis that arts and science female college students would differ significantly on their scores on achievement stress scale, academic stress scale, physical stress scale, family stress scale, social stress scale and total stress scale, was partially accepted. The two groups did differ significantly on frequency, quantity and total achievement stress; frequency of academic stress; frequency, quantity and total social stress; frequency, quantity and total stress score only, was accepted.
2. The hypothesis that under graduate and post graduate female college students would differ significantly on their scores on SAchs, SAS, SPS, SFS, SSS and total stress scale, was accepted.
3. The hypothesis that upper caste and lower caste female college students would differ significantly on their scores on SAchs, SAS, SPS, SFS, SSS and total stress scale, was

partially accepted. The two groups did differ significantly on SAchs, SAS, SFS, and total stress scale score only.

4. The hypothesis that high, middle and low economic level female college students would differ significantly on their scores on SAchs, SAS, SPS, SFS, SSS and total stress scale, was partially accepted. The three groups did differ significantly on frequency and total achievement stress score only.

5. The hypothesis that arts and science female college students would differ significantly on their scores on free floating anxiety, obsessive traits and sympotoms, phobic anxiety, somatic concomitants of anxiety, neurotic depressions, hysterical traits and symptoms and total MHQ scores, was partially accepted. The two groups did differ significantly on free floating anxiety, obsessive traits and symptoms, phobic anxiety, hysterical traits and total MHQ score only.

6. The hypothesis that under graduate and post graduate female college students would differ significantly on their scores on FFA, OBS, PHO, SOM, DEP and Total MHQ, was partially accepted. The two groups did differ significantly on FFA, SOM, DEP, HYS and total MHQ score only.

7. The hypothesis that upper caste and lower caste female college students would differ significantly on their scores on FFA, OBS, PHO, SOM, DEP, HYS and total MHQ, was accepted.

8. The hypothesis that high, middle and low economic level female college students would differ significantly on their scores on FFA, OBS, PHO, SOM, DEP, HYS and total MHQ, was partially accepted. The three groups did differ significantly on FFA, HYS only.

Descriptive findings

Who is most likely to be stressed?

It was hypothesized in the present study that several demographic factors might be related to student's perceptions of their stress level. Thus, it was analyzed whether there were differences in perceived stress by academic class, caste, curriculum and economic status. The present findings are totally significant for the level of education ,curriculum and caste. The majority of postgraduate students (64%, N=96) expressed feeling stress often, while in contrast, only 36% of undergraduate students (N=54) reported being stressed frequently. Lower caste students also perceived higher levels of stress. The vast majority (62.5%, N=63) of students who belonged to middle economic class being high levels of stress. Over a third (38%, N=57) of the low-stress group was from arts group.

Is stress related to the practice of other unhealthy behaviours?

The behaviour patterns of 'stressed' students are different from those of non-stressed students in several important ways. Those who experience high levels of stress are more likely to practice a number of unhealthy behaviors; like -over -eating,aggressiveness, lazy etc.

Do 'stressed' students experience reduced perceptions of health and self esteem?

Students who experience higher levels of stress also exhibit lower levels of satisfaction with their overall health. The percentage of 'stressed' students who perceive themselves as healthy (55.0%) is nearly equivalent to those who indicate that they are less healthy (45.0%). In contrast, those in the low stress group are significantly more likely to describe their health as 'excellent'or 'very good' (82.8%). These differences carry over into perceptions of self esteem as well. 'Stressed' students are significantly less satisfied with their GPA (Global Physical Appearances), weight and fitness level. Clearly, stressed students are much less satisfied with a variety of life factors that contribute to self-esteem. It remains unclear, however, whether high levels of stress reduce self-worth, or whether stress is a by-product of poor academic performance and higher level of neurotic behaviour.

The results suggest a relationship between perceived levels of stress among college students and neurotic behaviour. Students with high levels of stress tend to perceive themselves as less healthy, they possess lower levels of self-esteem and they are more prone to practice a number of poor health habits. There are several methodological concerns that may limit the generalizability of these results.

Recognizing effects of stress on girls

With nervous energy skyrocketing, the girls of this generation need the adults in their lives to do far more than in the past. Along with general understanding and support, they need voices of reason to counteract both the stress-inducing messages they get from this culture and the demoralizing, self-defeating beliefs some of them persist in telling themselves. But for this to happen, parents and teachers must first recognize the distress underlying the girl's attitude and behaviour.

Many signs of stress are so common that they are accepted as the normal, even expected, cost of leading busy, productive lives. What girls, for example, have not procrastinated in doing their proper study overreacted to a situation with a friend, or frozen while taking a test? What girl has not lost her temper, been moody, excessively tired, or occasionally used aches or pains as an excuse to stay home from college? It is the rare girl who has not taken out her troubles on a younger sibling or stayed up until all hours and then been late for school the next morning. Every parent and teacher should be aware of these basic truths about the insidious, sometimes devastating, effects of stress on girls throughout the college.

Girls are afflicted

The first thing adults need to know, is that stress for success is no longer exclusive to ambitious seniors, engaged in the nerve-racking college-application process. The epidemic in this culture has spread to ever-younger girls, infecting those on the cusp of puberty as well as older. Too often it is hear, the voices of girls who already feel very tired and defeated, though they have yet to graduate from the relatively protected confines of elementary school.

Intensify stress

From the time, girls enter the college developmental challenges exacerbate stress in every area. On the college front, girls are suddenly asked to follow mind-boggling rotating schedules, keep track of a slew of due dates, and deal with an array of teachers—each with their own preferences, idiosyncrasies, and expectations. This is the sort of juggling expected of corporate CEOs.

In general, girls feel desperate to reconnect with friends they may now see less frequently. They need to reassure themselves of these old ties by helping each other with problems and analyzing the details of all their unsettling social interactions. Well before they get to college, girls say they face daily dilemmas such as whether to get sleep or good grades, to work on math problems or friendship problems, and to study history. A generation ago, girls might have been playing Parcheesi, dressing up their Barbie dolls, and jumping rope. Today girls are obsessed with calculating their grade point averages, managing their time, and getting into good colleges and job.

Pressures skyrocket during college

When the stakes rise in college, so does the level of stress—for girls as well as their families the road to success is increasingly lined with specific checkpoints against which achievement is measured. For example, whether or not girls are in post graduation or advanced placement (AP) classes; whether their scores are high enough; whether they are chosen for selective subject or job; whether (and by whom) they are invited to problems and so on. Any one of these criteria can seem like the definitive word on whether or not girls are successful—or will be so in the future.

An undergraduate girl expressed about the pressures of many girls in graduation :

'The worst thing about graduation is the pressure to get into a good and desirable subject. My parents are pushing me to study harder. Plus, my friends pressured me to spend time with them, to go to their party or hang out. Have this boyfriend, you need one or you get stressed about home coming. It is a big deal. Are you going? Whom with? Do you have a dress? And with all these, I hope I get into a really good college and don't die from the stress of applying.'

Such issues may be common, even classic, during adolescence, but they are worse today, and suffering from stress should not be accepted. In fact, these are the harmful effects on girl's physical health and mental well-being and, therefore, on their ultimate success.

Sleep deprivation

Perhaps the most blatant consequence is the widespread lack of college girls among today. Though they require eight to ten hours of sleep per night, they generally get far less. Not surprisingly, when girls are asked about their worst college experiences, they typically speak of exhaustion:

- The stress, sleep deprivation, and depression that almost defined in first year.
- When the pressure comes on all in one week, result is very little sleep.
- Every time to work until two or three a.m. in the morning and then sit through class, the next day with a headache as time stops.
- Getting no sleep because of work, draining emotionally, physically, and mentally, and doing worse in college because of constant lack of sleep.

Girls are losing sleep because many are intentionally cheating themselves of sleep in order to do everything they need to do.

As a girl describes, "I'm staying up later and later to finish homework, or maybe I just want to read something for fun, go online, or relax, but I still have to wake up just as early in the morning and start the whole cycle again."

As girls often tell , "My mind go a mile a minute," "I'm too tired to fall asleep," and "I have too much going on." Regardless, whether they deliberately pull all-night to study or they toss and turn for hours in their beds, the fallout of sleep deprivation is the same.

Susceptibility to Stress and poor Mental health

Lack of sleep and the impairment in thinking ability that results, deprive girls of much needed skills to ward off the effects of stress. In addition, because of their compromised immune systems, they are more prone to illness. Getting sick and being absent from college cause additional stress because they miss key class work or tests, fall behind their classmates, and have to work harder to catch up others.

Increased craving for stimulants

Exhaustion also affects blood chemistry, provoking unhealthy cravings for caffeine, chocolate, sugar, and junk food (many girls would be horrified to learn that chronic sleepiness is associated with weight gain, which causes more stress).It is observed during the data collection that the majority of girls drank caffeinated beverages daily for extra energy.

Poorer coping ability

With a distinct lack of downtime, girls are less able to relax, sleep, read for pleasure, and exercise. This undermines their ability to combat both anxiety and depression. Similarly, without the benefit of solitary activities such as writing in journals, reading, and creating music or art, girls can not soothe themselves as well. Too much stressed out to take good care of themselves, they are that much less capable of dealing with tremendous stress.

Diminished brain power

Chronic stress also threatens girl's success more directlyby eroding their brainpower. Without the restorative and memory-building benefits of a restful night's sleep, girls can not concentrate or think as well, and they learn more slowly. In fact, researches show that staying up throughout the night results in the same level of mental acuity as being intoxicated above the legal limit for driving in most states. It is no wonder that sleep-deprived people performs many kinds of tasks poorly.

Also, emotions powerfully affect cognition. This relationship is the focus of much scientifi attention today. New methods of mapping brain activity are enabling neuro-scientists to understand how feelings and cognition interact in the brain. For example, one group of researchers discovered that mild emotional states such as amusement and anxiety affect college students' short-term memory. Neither emotional state nor the task alone made a difference.

Plummeting self-esteem

Chronic stress breeds feelings of inadequacy as well. Girls who find that they can not think clearly or perform well understandably lose confidence. Comparing themselves to the idealized role models that surround them in this culture, in their college, and even in their own families, many girls fear they will never measure up. They stop believing in themselves. They lose heart, not to mention motivation. Eventually, they stop trying.

Researches confirm that less successful students are self-handicapped. That is, they sabotage their performance by procrastinating, studying for shorter period of time, and barely reading their textbooks. This posture enables them to excuse their anticipated lack of excellence. If girls do not give their all and do poorly, they can blame lack of effort instead of lack of competence. Girls would rather be seen as lazy than stupid.

Thwarted success

There is one symptom of stress that few parents or teachers can overlook i.e. declining grades. The sheer number of hours girls spend in college, with all its simultaneous and complex social, emotional, and intellectual challenges, makes it likely that problems will show up there first. It is hard for the parents and teachers to dismiss, rationalize, or justify poor report. They are most often seen—and correctly so—as red flags for trouble, perhaps even as girls' unconscious requests for adults to sit up and take notice.

Less often, girls manage to hold it together, silently and cheerfully going about the business of meeting other people's expectations. These girls do not complain. In fact, they seem to do everything and to do it all easily. They are model students and perfect daughters, likely to elicit praise and gratitude from adults. In fact, they are often taken as examples for other girls to emulate that is, until they reach a breaking point.

It is worth stating not even a single girl gets through college unscathed. No girl is immune to experiencing problems. The crucial question for educators and parents, is then, to what degree girls are adversely affected or even incapacitated by stress. Given how well they hide their pain, how can we assume that when they seem to be doing okay they are *really* doing okay? How can we know when girl's unhappiness with their activities, friends, or teachers,their struggle in a particular subject or anxiety about their future is normal—and when we should be concerned? Which girls are at risk for full-blown crises?

Psychologists conducting research in the field of psychoneuroimmunology (PNI) may have some answers. According to a newly developed bio-psychosocial model of health and well being, unhealthy reactions to stress occur when life's demands overtax coping skills. Whether stress results in a lowered immune response, susceptibility to infection or depression depends on mitigating factors such as mental outlook, optimism, and social support. Perhaps most interesting, is the body's physiological responses to stress which depend more on *perceptions* of inner resources than on actual coping ability. It is whether girls *think* they can manage—that is, self-confidence—that matters most.

These findings are consistent with clinical experience. Girls go into crisis when they believe their pressures are unsurmountable. Whatever coping skills they have counted on in the past, no longer seem to work for them.

Guidance counsellors from across the country are reporting a sharp increase in psychological crisis among female students and, as a result, an overwhelming use of college resources.

National statistics confirms these anecdotal data. Serious mental health problems are not only increasing, but also occurring earlier in childhood. Obsessive-compulsive disorders among youth are also skyrocketing.

Many stressed-out girls are turning to risk-taking behaviors such as using substances and engaging in inappropriate sexual activity. As one school administrator told, "Girls who have to do well in college are very dutiful on the surface. They're not going to violate the dress code, for example. But their interior lives are much more buried. They get into a lot of dreadful things. Girls can give you all the informations about drugs and alcohol and sexual behaviors".

Although these girls are often thought of as troubled or rebellious, their behavior is actually best understood as attempts at self medicating for anxiety and despair. This may explain a disturbing trend. For the first time ever, girls are using mind-numbing substances such as alcohol and tobacco at the same rate as boys.

Equally worrisome, is that these vulnerabilities to stress do not end with graduation. Ironically, with all the mechanizations of trying to get girls accepted into college, they are not doing as well once they get there.

The Higher Educational Research Institute at UCLA, for example, found that the emotional well being of freshmen hit an all time low at the beginning of the 2001-2002 academic years, even before September 11, 2001. As an article on student wellness in the American Psychological Association's *Monitor on Psychology* described, "At campuses all across the country, more undergraduate and graduate students are reporting depression, substance use, eating disorders, learning disabilities, and, most common, problems adapting to college life." Indeed, a 2004 study of 47,200 college students, conducted by the American College Health Association found, that 45 percent reported feeling so depressed during the past school year that it was difficult for them to function.

In response, a new federal law was enacted in October 2004 to provide grants to universities to enhance mental health services on campuses. In addition to traditional therapies, colleges have begun to offer stressed-out students a variety of services—from massages to dog cuddling or biofeedback to stress-free zones.

But we have to do our part as well. To send off girls to college well prepared, we have to encourage them to develop healthier attitudes about achievement and better strategies for coping with stress. Once again, girls need more help in these areas.

Key findings

- Persistent gender expectations are being compounded by a growing emphasis on perfection, resulting in mounting pressure on girls to be perfect. Three-quarters of girls (76%) in the study agree that girls are under a lot of pressure to please everyone, and 84% of these girls say that they dislike.
- Girls (76%) say that they are under a great deal of stress today.
- Girls want to seize the opportunities available to them, with 71% of participants reporting that they aspire to go to college after graduating from high school. However, stress and concerns such as the cost of college undermine girls' quality of life, particularly as they get older.
- Support systems bolster girls' ability to believe they can achieve their dreams and endure stress, and yet, one in ten girls (10%) and one in five girls (20%) say that they do not know even three persons to whom to turn if they have a problem.
- Girls are specially frustrated by the limiting expectations facing, because these challenges echo their professional and social struggle.Six in ten(60%) believe that girls are under a lot of pressure to please everyone.

5

Summary and Conclusion

Introduction

In India, it is considered that a female child grows up in a stressful environment in most of the families, particularly lower and middle classes. The socio-psychological environment, right from the conception stage, is less enthusiastic to have the female child. Lately, the practice of female infanticide, in large parts of the country, has increased. There is increased discrimination for female children compared with the male children or compared with the brothers. The female children are consistently discouraged from taking initiative and considered to be less mentally or physically capable. As a result, activities such as learning to ride bicycle, or drive a car, lifting, climbing are discouraged and there is a high degree of tension associated in case the female children take more interest. The female children are expected to help in the house, engage less in scholastic activities, encouraged to learn music, painting. As a girl grows to adolescence, she is given, day and night, a feeling of burden, whereas boys with similar achievement, would be considered an asset rather than a liability. Even when she becomes an adult, over 20, she is not free to move about. In many cases, she is forbidden to pursue higher studies. She is made greatly conscious of her physical up keen.....her attractiveness, height, weight and development of the body. At every sphere of life, there are anxieties and fears about acceptance, adjustment and fulfillment.

The economic pressures in the recent years have forced many girls, even from higher strata of the economy, to go to work or engage in some remunerative activities to supplement their family budget.

Every research investigation has some unique problems, the solutions of which are achieved through a specific research programme. The ultimate aim of any research is the addition of some significant and original ideas to the previously constituted body of knowledge. The present study is also an humble effort to contribute some sort of new ideas in the area of stress - neurotic behaviour relationship, the success of which is expected to expand the volume of stress and neurotic behaviour knowledge.

Effects of stress

1. There is a declining sex ratio since 1901. According to 1991 census there are 929 females/1000 males.
2. The mortality in females is higher than in males in all ages, and more marked in under five children. This is due comparatively to poorer nutritional status of female children, more respiratory diseases, less access to health services, neglected during illness.
3. Comparatively lesser number of female children, in spite of their better scholastic achievements, pursue higher education and go to professional and technical schools.
4. Comparatively lesser number of females, compared to males, become entrepreneurs, which requires risk-taking behaviour.
5. Suicide rate in females, compared to the males, is higher in high school students, college students, before marriage and five years after marriage.

6. The maternal mortality rate is higher in natal and postnatal complications are higher in women, experiencing greater social and cultural stresses.
7. More women experience psychiatric problems and are institutionalized, compared to males.

Objectives

The main aim of the present investigationo is to study the impact of certain psycho-social variables on stress and neurotic behaviour . The specific aims of the study were to :

1. find out the effect of curriculum, level of education, caste and economic level of female college students on stress, and
2. ascertain the influence of curriculum, level of education, caste and economic level of female college students on neurotic behaviour.

Hypotheses

The following hypotheses were framed for the study :

(1) The arts and science female college students would differ significantly on their scores on Achievement Stress Scale, Academic Stress Scale, Physical Stress Scale Family Stress Scale, Social Stress Scale and total Stress Scale.

(2) The under graduate and post graduate female college students would differ significantly on their scores on SAchs, SAS, SPS, SFS, SSS and total Stress Scale.

(3) The upper caste and lower caste female college students would differ significantly on their scores on SAchs, SAS, SPS, SFS, SSS and total Stress Scale.

(4) The high, middle and low economic level female college students would differ significantly on their scores on SAchs, SAS, SPS, SFS SSS and total stress scale.

(5) The arts and science female college students would differ significantly on their scores on Free Floating Anxiety,

obsessive traits and symptoms, phobic anxiety, somatic concomitants of anxiety, neurotic depression, hysterical traits and symptoms and total mhq.

(6) The under graduate and post graduate female college students would differ significantly on their scores on FFA, OBS, PHO, SOM,DEP,HYS and total MHQ.

(7) The upper caste and lower caste female college students would differ significantly on their scores on FFA,OBS,PHO,SOM,DEp,HYS and total MHQ.

(8) The high, middle and low economic level female college students would differ significantly on their scores on FFA, OBS, PHO, SOM, DEp, HYS and total MHQ.

Sample

The sample for the study consisted of 300 unmarried, semi-urban female students of normal physical health of Mahatma Gandhi Kashi Vidyapith University, Varanasi (U.P.), Udai Pratap College, Varanasi (U.P.) and Agrasen Mahajani Post Graduate College, Varanasi (U.P.). Only those subjects, who were interested in the research programme, and also those who had committed themselves for being co-operative for the entire programme, were included in the study. The subjects were selected purposively on the basis of curriculum, level of education, caste and economic level. Of the 300 subjects, 150 to science group, 150 to arts group; 150 subjects belonged to under graduate classes, 150 to post graduate classes; 144 belonged to upper caste and 137 to lower caste; 103 to high economic group, 128 to middle economic group and 69 to low economic group. Caste of some subjects could not be clearly ascertained in case of a few subjects of the total sample, and hence such cases, were dropped. The economic level was determined on the basis of income of the subjects. The high income group was ascribed to those subjects who full at Q_3 and above of the distribution, the low income group was labelled to those who were at and below Q_1 of the distribution and the remaining subjects formed middle income group. The age of the subjects ranged from 17 to 26 years with a mean of 24.3 years.

Measurement of variables

Stress and neurotic behaviour of the subjects were assessed with the help of Bisht Battery of Stress Scale (Bisht, 1987) and Middlesex Hospital Questionnaire (Crown and Crisp, 1966). Hindi version of MHQ was prepared by Srivastava and Bhatt in 1973. The other relevant details of the subjects were found out through the General Introductory Schedule developed for the purpose.

The study had the following dependent and independent variables –

Dependent variables :

(1) Stress

(2) Neurotic behaviour

Independent variables :

(1) Curriculum (Science and Arts)

(2) Level of Education (Under Graduate and Post Graduate)

(3) Caste (Upper caste and Lower caste)

(4) Economic level (High, Middle and Low)

The data were analysed for the four groups *viz.*, (i) science and arts, (ii) under graduate and post graduate (iii) upper caste and lower caste (iv) high, middle and low economic level female college students on two variables *viz.*, stress and neurotic behaviour, adopting 't' test and 'F' test of significance. The Stress had five sub-areas *viz.*, achievement stress, academic stress, physical stress, social stress, family stress and one total score. Neurotic behaviour had six sub-areas *viz.*, free floating anxiety obsessive traits and symptoms, phobic anxiety, somatic concomitants of anxiety, neurotic depression, hysterical traits and symptoms and one total score.

Conclusions

On the basis of findings of two groups *viz.*, arts and science on various aspects of BBSS, following conclusions were drawn :

(1) The arts and science female college students did differ significantly on the frequency, quantity and total achievement stress; frequency of academic stress; frequency, quantity and total social stress; frequency, quantity and total family stress; frequency, quantity and total stress. The arts students obtained higher mean values than those of the science students.

(2) The two groups in question, however did not differ significantly on the quantity and total academic stress; frequency, quantity and total physical stress.

On the basis of findings of two groups *viz.* under graduate and post graduate on the various aspects of BBSS following conclusions were drawn :

The under graduate and post graduate female college students did differ significantly on the frequency, quantity and total achievement stress; frequency, quantity and total academic stress; frequency, quantity and total physical stress; frequency, quantity and total social stress; frequency, quantity and total family stress; frequency, quantity and total stress. The post graduate students have higher mean values than those of the under graduate students.

On the basis of findings of two groups viz., upper caste and lower caste female college students on total BBSS and its various aspects following conclusions were drawn:

(1) The upper caste and lower caste female college students did differ significantly on the frequency, quantity and total achievement stress; frequency, quantity and total academic stress; frequency, quantity and total family stress; frequency, quantity and total social stress, frequency-quantity and grandtotal stress. The lower caste students have higher mean values than thoes of the upper caste students.

(2) The two groups in question, however, did not differ significantly on the one aspect *viz.*, frequency, quantity and total physical stress.

On the basis of findings of three groups *viz.*, high, middle and low economic level female college students on the various aspects of BBSS, following conclusions were drawn:

(1) The three groups in question *viz.*, high, middle and low economic level female college students did differ significantly on the frequency of achievement stress and total achievement stress.

(2) The three groups in question, however, did not differ significantly on the quantity of achievement stress; frequency, quantity and total academic stress; frequency, quantity and total physical stres; frequency, quantity and total social stress; frequency, quantity and total family stress as well as on grand total stress.

The following conclusions were drawn after comparing the mean scores of arts and science female college students on MHQ and its sub-tests :

(1) The arts and science female college students had significantly different mean scores on free floating anxiety, obsessive traits and symptoms, phobic anxiety, hysterical traits and total MHQ scores. Arts students obtained higher mean values than thoes of science students.

(2) The arts and science female college students did not differ significantly on their mean values of somatic concomitants of anxiety and neurotic depression. This difference in mean values had come due to chance factor.

On the basis of findings of study on two groups *viz.*, post graduate and under graduate on the various aspects of MHQ, following conclusions were drawn:

(1) The post graduate and under graduate female college students did differ significantly on free floating anxiety, somatic concomitants of anxiety, neurotic depression

hysterical traits and symptoms as well as on total MHQ scores. The post graduate students obtained higher mean values than those of the under graduate students.

(2) The post graduate and under graduate female college students however did not differ significantly on two aspects *viz.*, obsessive traits and symptoms and phobic anxiety.

The following conclusions were drawn after comparing mean scores of upper caste and lower caste female college students on various aspects of mhq :

The upper caste and lower caste female college students did differ significantly on free floating anxiety, obsessive traits and symptoms, phobic anxiety, somatic concomitants of anxiety, neurotic depression, hysterical traits and total mhq scores. The lower caste students obtained higher mean values than those of the upper caste students.

The following conclusions were drawn after comparing mean scores of high, middle, and low economic level female college students on mhq and its sub-tests :

(1) the high, middle and low economic level female college students did differ significantly on free floating anxiety and hysterical traits and symptoms.

(2) the three groups, in question, however did not differ significantly on obsessive traits and symptoms, phobic anxiety, somatic concomitants of anxiety, neurotic depression and total mhq.

Hypothesis-wise general conclusions

On the basis of findings of study following general conclusions were drawn hypothesis-wise :

(1) The hypothesis that arts and science female college students would differ significantly on their scores on achievement stress scale, academic stress scale, physical stress scale, family stress scale, social stress scale and total stress scale, was partially accepted. The two groups

did differ significantly on the frequency-quantity and total achievement stress; frequency of academic stress; frequency, quantity and total social stress; frequency, quantity and total family stress; frequency, quantity and total stress score only.

(2) The hypothesis that under graduate and post graduate female college students would differ significantly on their scores on SAchs, SAS, SPS, SFS, SSS and total stress scale, was accepted.

(3) The hypothesis that upper caste and lower caste female college students would differ significantly on their scores on SAchs, SAS, SPS, SFS, SSS and total stress scale, was partially accepted. The two groups did differ significantly on SAchs, SAS, SFS, SSS and total stress scale score only.

(4) The hypothesis that high, middle and low economic level female college students would differ significantly on their scores on SAchs, SAS, SFS, SSS and total stress scale, was partially accepted. The three groups did differ significantly on the frequency and total achievement stress score only.

(5) The hypothesis that arts and science female college students would differ significantly on their scores on free floating anxiety, obsessive traits and symptoms, phobic anxiety, somatic concomitants of anxiety, neurotic depression, hysterical traits and symptoms and total MHQ scores, was partially accepted. The two groups did differ significantly on free floating anxiety, obsessive traits and symptoms, phobic anxiety, hysterical traits and total MHQ score only.

(6) The hypothesis that under graduate and post graduate female college students would differ significantly on their scores on FFA, OBS, PHO, SOM, DEP, HYS and Total MHQ, was partially accepted. The two groups did differ significantly on FFA, SOM, DEP, HYS and Total MHQ score only.

(7) The hypothesis that upper caste and lower caste female college students would differ significantly on their scores on FFA, OBS, PHO, SOM, DEP, HYS and total MHQ, was accepted.

(8) The hypothesis that high, middle and low economic level female college students would differ significantly on their scores on FFA, OBS, PHO, SOM, DEP, HYS and Total MHQ, was partially accepted. The three groups did differ significantly on FFA, HYS only.

Key findings

- Persistent gender expectations are being compounded by a growing emphasis on perfection, resulting in mounting pressure on girls to be very perfect. Three-quarters of girls (76%) in the study agree that girls are under a lot of pressure to please everyone, and 84% of these girls say that they dislike it.
- Girls(76%) say they are under a great deal of stress today.
- Girls want to seize the opportunities available to them, with 71% of participants reporting that they aspire to go to college full time after graduating from high school. However, stress and concerns such as the cost of college undermine girl's quality of life, particularly as they get older.
- Support systems bolster girl's ability to believe that they can achieve their dreams and endure stress, and yet one in ten girls (1%) and one in five high school girls (20%) say that they do not know three adults to whom to turn if they have a problem.
- Girls and boys face different stereotypes, and concerns-girls are expected to be the nurturers and care takers; 84% of girls and 87% of boys believe girls are 'supposed to be kind and caring'. Boys, on the other hand, are expected to be protectors; 88% of girls and 94% of boys believe that

boys are 'supposed to be able to protect themselves and others.'

- Women are especially frustrated by the limiting expectation-facing girls, because these challenges echo their professional and social struggles. Eight out of ten girls (84%) believe that girls are under a lot of pressure to please everyone; 91% of these girls dislike that this is true.

'Society still sees girls through a gender lens that requires them to be adjustable and passive, while increasingly expecting girls to be smart and successful. The findings underscore the need to pay close attention and deconstruct the messages, girls receive in and outside of their home,' says Joyce M. Roche, President and CEO of Girls Inc. 'We have to acknowledge girls' concerns, contributions, and experiences and help them be 'super' in ways that are comfortable and healthy.'

The study makes it clear that girls are internalizing our culture's conflicting and unrealistic expectations of girls and women. Particularly troubling is the overemphasis on physical perfection, even at very young ages. Half of the girls in grades 3-5 (54%) and three-quarters of the girls in grades 6-8 (74%) and grades 9-12 (76%) report that they worry about their appearance. 'Even today,' sums up one 9th grade girl, 'society values beauty in girls over intelligence and talent.'

The study examines the implications of the findings and offers recommendations for addressing the issues raised by the data. Here, too, girls themselves offer cogent directions. 'It is hard to live up to what everyone wants for us,' says post graduate girl. 'We need to do things at our own pace and in our own time. And just believe in us; support us as we grow up.'

Girls Grapple with the Mounting Pressure of Expectations, a research report from Girls , reveals that girls today experience intense pressure, at ever younger ages, to be everything to everyone all of the time. Girls are particularly frustrated with the growing expectations that girls should please everyone, be very homely as well academic and dress 'right.' There are so many pressures of being a girl,'told a science graduate.

Social implication of the findings

The findings of this research have got great social implications. The female, in the established typical Indian social framework, are the nucleus of the family system and transcripter of social values and norms. They are the womb bearer of the civilization and scripter of the stories of the great socio-cultural and economic change.

In spite of having such an important role to play regarding the socio-cultural reforms, the female, in general is having a lot of psycho-social problems, not only at a matured age but also at the student age level. This study brings forward a qualitative and quantitative measure of the various stresses associated with them and at the student level age group. Irrespective of their social status (the variables being curriculum, level of education, and economic level), they are generally having achievement, academic, physical, family and social stresses associated with them which, needless to say, go on increasing in due course. This leads to such a complex situations when she is having a very conferred mental status because of high level of role ambiguity and role conflict, leading ultimately to highly stressed, puzzled and under developed personalities who find themselves unable to discharge their family and social responsibilities.

This study also gives a chance for an introspection to the sociologist and psychologist who talk much of women empowerment and development. The various NGO's and Government agencies, who are planning and executing various women empowerment and development programmes, should take note of these findings while assessing their mental status.

It can, therefore, be concluded with the opinion that mental health of the female at such an premature age is alarmingly stressed and need to be paid serious attention if we relly want to make them participate in the socio-economic and cultural changes, that are due to take place in the coming future.

Future strategy

First, the relationship between gender and stress among college female students is one that is well-documented in the literature. Programmes to address traditionally 'female' issues, such as anorexia, are commonly found on college campuses nationwide. The findings suggest that it may be useful to develop gender-specific programmes targeted at reducing the general level of stress among female college students. Further research should consider the unique sources of stress among college females. Is it that the sources of stress for college females are different, or do college-aged females have distinct, and perhaps less effective ways of handling stress? The answer to this question would facilitate the development of programmes that are more effectively targeted to address the particular needs and coping skills of college female and male students.

The finding that high levels of stress are associated with neurotic behaviour is not startling when considered in the context of the literature on stress within the adult population. In the population at large, higher levels of stress have been related to poor diet, erratic sleep patterns and increased levels of stress-related illness, e.g., heart attacks. High levels of stress have also been linked to a variety of psychological ailments in the college-aged population, e.g., suicide ideation (Hirsch and Ellis, 1996). Further research with college students might document the extent to which "stressed" students experience other sorts of physical illnesses more frequently. It may be useful to understand the long-term effects of stress on students' stamina.

It is likely that students experience a series of non-acute ailments, perhaps both physical and psychological, before they seek health care interventions. With an increased understanding of the mechanisms that students use to cope with stress, programmes might be better designed to alleviate the effects of stress at an earlier point, before more severe consequences arise.

Further research might also study the stress reduction patterns of students for whom stress is not a concern. How and why are some students able to maintain lower stress levels? What strategies do they use for reducing stress? Are the stressors they experience unique in some way, or are they simply avoiding issues that create stress for other students? Research targeted at understanding the practices and attitudes of these students may provide valuable information that may be used to help students who are more susceptible to stress.

Limitations of the present study

1. The study is limited to Varanasi (U.P.) and among semi-urban female college students.
2. The study is concerned with arts and science female college students. It may be extended to :
   (a) Female college students on a larger sample.
   (b) A comparative study on stress and neurotic behaviour among married and unmarried female college students.
   (c) A comparative study on the stress and neurotic behaviour among urban and rural female college students.
3. Similar studies might be refunded to male student population.

Seniors (postgraduate students), however, are also subject to unique types of stress in the present study. The study was conducted during mid session. Many seniors were in the midst of finishing large final papers and finalizing career or other post-graduate plans. Thus, the timing at which the study was conducted might have influenced our findings, as they pertain to seniors. In contrast, the stress levels of other students may have been artificially low when the survey was given. Students typically have few major assignments during this time, and most have been relaxing, catching up on sleep and completing assignments. Thus, they may perceive their work load as more manageable than at other time points during the year.

Achievements

Suggestions to cope with stress in life

These suggestions are at two levels – environmental and individual levels. Certain changes in the attitudes and systems would be required which will create an environment for optimism, fulfillment and adjustment of females. Individual level programmes will differ from individual to individual, keeping in view the cognitive, emotive and behavioural capacities.

A. Environmental

1. For the girl child survival and quality of life, the Government and voluntary organizations should aim at improving the social acceptance of the female child. This could be achieved through mass education of the public to accept the children as children, irrespective of the sex.
2. The parents should seek health services for female children as for the male children. The Government health services should be more accessible concessional basis, health services for female children.
3. There should be reservation of quotas for admission for female children in schools and colleges. More scholarships from Government Foundations and Trusts should offer scholarships to female children with scholastic achievements and creative potentials.

4. There should be reservation of quotas for employment in public and private organizations.
5. Government and voluntary organizations should carry out mass awareness programmes for parents of the boys and young men not to demand, even not to accept, any dowry. Social sanctions should be exercised against those who demand dowry.
6. Counseling services should be available from the Department of Women's Welfare and voluntary organizations for emotional, social and economic adjustment.
7. Mass communication programmes should be designed for males to help in household work, taking care of the children, and other related activities.

B. Individual level

1. Making priorities clear- Most of the females experience conflict since one or the other aspects of life has to be sacrificed or suffers. This is a personal decision as to what ultimately an individual wants and what type of identity a person wants to maintain.
2. Define Goals and Objectives- More the goals and objectives are clear with regard to marriage, occupation and achievements in life, less will be the stresses or conflicts an individual will have to experience. Many girls, even the boys, really would not like to get married but do get married only to avoid social pressures. These girls, who never wanted to get married, are more career-oriented, are likely to experience greater stresses unless they internalize the need for marriage and resolve the internal conflicts.
3. Career pursuit does not necessarily mean being engaged in an occupation or activity, which is remunerative, and that one has to be satisfied only in the context of an

employment. Many girls can satisfy their creative and personal interest by engaging in activities such as writing, painting, music, tuition at home, social service and sharing experiences with others.

4. Be determining to cope with stress- One of the ways to cope with stress is to get into stress. In other words, face and fight the situation rather than run away or regress in a situation. At home, at school and in the environment there will be people who may talk about and laugh at the behaviours whenever a girl or woman takes the initiative. Long time ago, Thomas Carlyle wrote, 'every creative idea or a bold initiative will be laughed at, criticized and considered by people as impossible; but when achieved, the same people would admire and appreciate'. Today, we have an excellent atmosphere in the country, better than in any other country, for becoming an entrepreneur or pursuing personal interests. Initiative is required. Initial resistance, failures, criticisms or insecurities will soon turn into success, confidence and achievements, if the female would stick to the decisions and go ahead with the initiative taken.

5. Personal up dating: Whether remaining at home during raising the children, or on the job, to compete successfully in the social and economic environment, the women should update their knowledge and skill. This can be attained through formal and informal training, reading and taking courses. Large numbers of such programmes are being offered to day by the private, voluntary and Governmental organizations. The Indira Gandhi National Open University is a unique institution in the world (no other country has such programmes which are available through print and audio-video media). There are nearly 50 different programmes of short and long duration. As Mahatma Gandhi used to say "knowledge is power;

knowledge gives character and character becomes power"; with increased competence, women would be able to compete success fully with their male counterparts who would give them confidence and acceptance. The Information Technology industry has opened up great opportunities for all, particularly for women. After some training many of them can work outside or start service at home. Many young women have become very successful entrepreneurs.

6. Regular Physical Exercises and Yoga: Whether working or non-working, besides the physical activities at home required in house hold work, women should engage themselves in regular physical exercises, yoga, breathing exercises, long morning and evening walks, preferably with children. In addition, they should have proper balanced diet. These will help them being physically fit and they will remain active and attractive like the Western counterparts until later years of their lives.

Contribution to further research

The present research is a micro study of a very complex phenomenon.The following suggestions may be of some use for further study in this area:

(1) This study provides a base line data for the research workers to carry out a longitudinal study in future.

(2) The present study is confined to the non-tribal community only. It is therefore, suggested that the research workers may conduct a study on the tribal sample which may reveal neurotic behaviour that they are facing due to the undergoing process of stress.For the sake of understanding a comparative picture of the impact of stress on the mental health of the tribal and non-tribal groups, a future study is needed.

(3) Researches are also required to be made as to why the religion has a significant effect on the stress and neurotic behaviour among college girls, while the same has no role to play in case of stress and neurotic behaviour among female college students.

Finally, stress may be place-specific. This study was undertaken in various college and university of Varanasi city of Uttar Pradesh. The perceived level of expectations regarding girl's performance is high. The majority of the student body will pursue graduate study in some field. The environment here is one that fosters academic and extra-curricular excellence. As such, the prevalence of stress among the students may be exceptionally high, and some of our findings may not be applicable to students in less competitive academic settings.

Bibliography

Aldwin, C. M. 1994. *Stress, coping, and development: An integrative perspective.* New York: Guilford Press.

Alpert, R. and R.M.Haber 1960. Anxiety in academic achievement situation. *Journal of Abnormal and Social Psychology.* 61: 207-215.

Avila, C. 1994. Facilitation and inhibition of visual orienting as a function of personality. *Personality and Individual Difference.* 18(4) : 503-509.

Bancroft, J. *et al.* 1994. Vulnerability to premenstrual mood change : The relevance of a past history of depressive disorder. *Psychosomatic Medicine.* 56 (3) : 225-231.

Basowitz, H., S.J. Kordein, and R.R. Grinker 1995. *Anxiety and Stress : An interdisciplinary study of a life situation.* New York : Mc Graw Hill.

Beitman, B.1993. Source of occupational stress in school phycologists, *Dissertation Abstracts International.* 44(3) : 705.

Bertolotti, G. *et al.* 1995. Psychophysiological reactivity, depression, neuroticism and Type A behaviour : An introductive effect ? *Stress Medicine.* II(2) : 123-129.

Berenbaum, H. and M. Williams 1995. Personality and Emotional reactivity. *Journal of Research in Personality*. 29(I) : 24-34.

Bendien, J. and J.Groen 1963. A Psychological statistical study of neuroticism and extraversion in patients with myocardial infraction. *Journal of Psychosomatic Research*. 7.

Breslan, N,H.D. Chilcoat and P. Andreski, 1996. Further evidence on the link between migraine and neuroticism. *Neurology*. 47(3): 663-667.

Bridges, P.K. and M.T. Jones 1967.Personality, Physique and the adrenocortical response to Psychological Stress. *British Journal of Psychiatry*.113.

Bronner, R.L.1987. Towards a predictive model of suicidal ideation and behaviour : Some preliminary data in college students. *Suicidal Life Threat Behaviour*. 17(1): 50-63.

Bronner, R.L.1987. Concurrent validity of a stress-vulnerability model of suicidal ideation and behaviour A follow-up study. *Suicide Life Threat Behaviour*. 17(1) : 265-270.

Bronner, R.L. 1988. A prospective investigation of suicidal ideation in college students : A test of a model. *Suicide Life Threat Behaviour*. 18(3) : 245-258.

Brown, K. W. and Moskowitz. 1997. Does unhappiness make you sick? The role of affect and neuroticism in the experience of comment physical symptoms. *Journal of Personality and Social Psychology*. 72 (4) :907-917.

Byrne *et al.* 1995. Personality, stress and the decision to commence cigarette smoking in adolescence. *Journal of Psychosomatic Research*. 39(1) : 53-62.

Cattle, R.B.1946. *Description and measurement of Personality.* Yonkers – on – Hudson : World Books.

Cattel, R.B.1965. *The sciencetific analysis of personality.* Penguin Books Ltd.

Chaudhary, B.K.and R.B. Sinha. 1992. A study of adjustment in relation to some personality factors. *Indian Journal of Psychometry and Education.* 23(1) : 36-36B.

Christensen, H.J. *et al.*1993 Neuroticism and the belief that one is being scrutinized and evaluated by others. *Personality and Individual Difference.* 15(3) : 349-350.

Coates, D. B. 1970. Yorklea Social Environment Survey. (Technical Report) Toronto: Clarke Institute of Psychiatry.

Coates, D. B. 1972. *Yorklea Study Final Report.*

Coates, D. B., Kendall, L. M., MaCurdy, E. A., Goodacre, R. H. 1976. Evaluating hospital and home treatment for psychiatric patients. *Canada's Mental Health, March.*

Codrane,R.1969. Neuroticism and discovery of high blood pressure. *Journal of Psychosomatic Research.* 13.

Coleman, James. C.1974. *Abnormal Psychology and Modern Life* (3rd Edition) Bombay : D.B. Taraporevala Sons and Co.

Cramer, Duncan.1993. Personality, socio-economic status and age disparity in marriage. *Personality and Individual Differences.* 15(6) : 725-727.

Croog, S. H. 1970. The family as a source of stress. In S. Levine & N. A. Scotch (Eds.), *Social stress.* Chicago: Aldine Press.

Dill, Patricia L. and Tracey B. Henley 1998. Stressors of College: A Comparison of Traditional and Nontraditional Students. *Journal of Psychology,* 132(1): 25-32.

Driskell and Olenstead.1991. Effects of stress on group performance. *Journal of Clinical Psychology.* 49 (3).

Duggau, C. *et al.*1995. Neuroticism : A vulnerability marker for depression evidence from a family study. *Journal of Affective Disorders.* 35(3) : 139-143.

D'Zurilla, T.J. and C.F.Sheedy, 1991.Relation between social problem-solving ability and subsequent level of psychological stress in college students. *Journal Perspective of Social Psychology.* 61(5) : 841- 846.

Eastham, K., Coates, D. B., & Allodi, F. 1970. 'The concept of crisis: An expository review. *Canadian Psychiatric Association Journal,* 15, 463-472.

Ensel, Walter M., and Nan Lin. 1991. The life stress paradigm and psychological distress. *Journal of Health and Social Behaviour.* 32: 321-341.

Epstein, S. and L. Katz, 1992.Coping ability, stress, productive load and symptoms. *Journal Perspective of Social Psychology.* 62(5) : 813-825.

Eysenck, H.J.1947. *Dimensions of Personality.* London : Routledge and Kegan Paul.

Eysenck, H.J. 1967. *The Biological Basis of Personality.* Spring Field : Thomas.

Eysenck, H. J. and S.B.G. Eysenck, 1969. *Personality Structure and Measurement.* London : Routledge and Kegan Paul.

Eysenck, H.J.1970. *Structure of Human Personality.* London: The London, Methuen and Co. Ltd.

Eysenck, H.J. and M.W. Eysenek, 1985.*Personality and Individual Differences : A Natural Science Approach.* New York: Plenum.

Freud, S. 1920. *General Introduction of Psychoanalysis.* New York : Linernright.

Freud, S.1954. *The Origins of Psychoanalysis.* New York,.

Felsten, G. 1991. Influences of situation specific mastery beliefs and satisfaction with social support on appraisal of stress. *Psychological Report.* 69(2) : 483-495.

Francis, Les Li e J. 1993. The dual nature of the Eysenckian Neuroticism Scales : A Question of Sex Differences. *Personality and Individual Differences.* 15(1) : 43-59.

Friedman, *et al.*1994. Post traumatic stress disorder in the military veteran. *Psychiatric Clinics of North America.* 17(2) : 265-277.

Garrison, C.Z.1989. The study of suicidal behaviour in the schools. *Suicidal Life Threat Behaviour.* 19(1) : 120-130.

Garrett, H.E.1966. *Statistics in Psychology and Education. New* York : David Mckey Company Inc.

Goldenson, Robert M. *The Encyclopedia of Human Behaviour. Vol. I & II* New York, Double Day & Co.

Gotham, H.J., K.J. Sher, and P.K. Wood. 2003. Alcohol involvement and developmental task completion during young adulthood. *Journal of Studies of Alcoholism.* 64 : 15-22.

Gray, J.1971. *The Psychology of Fear and Stress.* London : Neidenfeld and Nicolson, New York. McGraw Hill.

Grinker R.R. and J.P.Spiegel, 1945. *Menunder Stress.* Philadelphia : Blackiston.

Gupta, U. and B.S.Gupta, 1994. Effect of Caffeine on perceptual judgement : A dose-response study special Issue : Caffeine Research. *Phormacopsychoe Cologia.*

Gupta, A. and S.Sharma, 1987. Effect of trait anxiety intelligence and psychological stress on state anxiety. *Indian Psychological Review.* 4 : 35-45.

Harris *et al.*1991. Effects of stress on human performance. *Journal of Clinical Psychology.* 49(3).

Heckman and Marris,1991. A study of flight crew performance. *Journal of Clinical Psychology.* 49(3).

Herbart, P.G.1952. The measurement of family relationships. *Human Relation.* 5(1) : 3-30.

Hirsch, Jameson K. and Jon B. Ellis. 1996. Differences in life stress and reasons for living among college suicide ideators and nonideators. *College Student Journal,* 30 (3): 377-386.

Hovanitz, C.A.1986. Life events stress and coping style as contributors to Psychopathology. *Journal of Clinical Psychology.* 42(I) : 34-41.

Irmis, F.1995. Roation of extraversion and neuroticism to E.E.G. alpha indicators : Four extreme groups. *Studia Psychology.* 36(5) : 282-284.

Jou, Y.H. and H. Fukada, 1997. Stress and social - support in mental and physical health of Chinese students in Japan. *Psychological Report.* 81(3pt 2): 1303-1312.

Jung, J and H.K.Khalsa, 1989. The relationship of daily hassless, social support and coping to depression in black and white students. *Journal of General Psychology.* 116(4) : 407-417.

Kentle, R.L. 1997. Elements of neuroticism in relation to headache symptomatology. *Psychological Report.* 80(1): 227-235.

Kissin, B.1974. The Pharmacodynamics and natural history of alcoholism. In B. Kissin, and H. Begleiter, (eds.) *The biology of alchoholism.* Vol. 3. *Clinical Pathology,* New York : Plemm.

Kisker, G.W.1972. *The Disorganized Personality.* Mc Graw Hill Kogakusha Ltd.

Kisker, G.W.1985. *The Disorganized Personality* (3rd Ed) Toronto, Condo : Mc Graw Hill Book Company.

Kleimutz, B. 1967. *Personality measurement : An Introduction.* Homewood, III : Dorsey Press.

Laughlin, H .P. 1967. *The Neuroses* Washington, Butterworths.

Lau, Richard R., Marilyn Jacobs Quadrel and Karen A. Hartman. 1990. Development and Change of Young Adults' Preventive Health Beliefs and Behavior: Influence from Parents and Peers. *Journal of Health and Social Behaviour,* 31: 240-59.

Lazarus, R.S. 1963. *Personality and Adjustment.* Prentice Hall.

Lee, K.A. *et al.*1995. A 50-year Perspective study of the psychological sequential of World War-II Combat. *American Journal of Psychiatry.* 152(4) : 516-522.

Lepore, S.J.1992. Social Conflict, Social-Support and Psychological Distress : Evidence of cross-domain buffering effects. *Journal Perspective of Social Psychology.* 63(5) : 857-867.

Lepore, *et al.*1993. Social-support lowers cordiovascular reactivity to an acute stressor. *Psychosomatic Medicine.* 55(6) : 518-524.

Lepore, S.J.1995. Lynicism, social support and cardiovascular reactivity. *Health Psychology.*14(3).

Levi, L. 1967. (Ed.) *Emotional Stress.* Basel S. Karger.

Liebart, R.M. and L.W. Morris, 1983. Influence of family system, life change stress on behavioural adjustment of early adolescents. *Dissertation Abstract international.* 44(1) : 376.

Lynn, R. and T. Martine, 1995. National differences for thirty-seven nations in extroversion-neuroticism, psychoticism. *Personality and Individual Differences.* 19(3) : 403-406.

Lynn, R. and T. Martine, 1997. Gender differences in extroversion, neuroticism, and psychoticism in 37 nations. *Journal of Social Psychology.* 137(3) : 369-373.

Maqnus, K. *et al.*1993. Extraversion and neuroticism as predicators objective life events : A longitudinal analysis. *Journal of Personality and Social Psychology.* 65(5) : 1946-1953.

Murray, G.W. *et al.* 1995. Personality factors in seasonal affective disorder : Is seasonality an aspect of neuroticism. *Personality and Individual Differences.* 19(5) : 613-617.

Marincola, L.B. and G.M. Long, 1985. Perceptual style and dual-task performance as a function of task difficulty and task emphasis. *Perceptual and Motor Skills.* 61(3) (pt.2) : 1092-1105.

Martine, W.1983. Influences of family system, life change stress on behavioural adjustment of early adolescents. *Dissertation Abstract International.* 44(3).

Mangan, G.L. *et al.*1993. Photic driving and personality. *Personal and Individual differences.* 15(3) : 329-340.

McCormack, Arlene Smith. 1996. Drinking in stressful situations: college men under pressure. *College Student Journal,* 30 (1): 65-77.

Mc Dougall *et al.*1988. Smoking, caffeine, and stress : Effects on blood pressure and heart rate in male and female college students. *Health Psychology.* 7(5) : 461-478.

Mc Grath, J.E.1970. *A conceptual formulation for research on stress,* New York.

Mc Kenzie, J. and G.Tindell, 1993. Anxiety and Academic Achievement : Further Furneaux Factor Findings. *Personal and Individual Differences.* 15(6) : 607-617.

Megel, Mary Erickson, Peggy Hawkins, Susie Sandstrom, Mary Ann Hoefler, and Kathleen Willrett. 1994. Health Promotion, Self-Esteem and Weight Among Female College Freshman. *Health Values,* 18 (4): 10-19.

Minugh, P.A. and L.L.Harlow. 1994. Substance use clusters multi–theoretical approach. *Journal of Substance Abuse.* 6(1) : 45-66.

Morgan, Sue. 1997. "Cheap drinks, heavy costs: students and alcohol." *Youth and Policy,* 56: 42-54.

Morris *et al.*1995. Personality neuroticism and depression after stroke. *International Journal of Psychiatry in Medicine.* 25(1) : 93-103.

Moss, Gordon E. 1973. *Illness Immunity and Social Interaction.* New York: John Wiley.

Mowrer, O.H.1950. *Learning Theory and Personality Dynamics.* New York : Renold.

Mwamwenda, T.S.1995. Associations with neuroticism and introversion with academic achievement. *Psychological Report.* 77(1) : 265-266.

Myers, V.D. *et al.*1995. Neuroticism : A position paper. *Journal of Psychological Type.* 35 : 3-9.

Nattiv, Aurielia and James C. Puffer 1991. Lifestyle and Health Risk of Collegiate Athletes. *The Journal of Family Practice*, 33 (6): 585-90.

Naquin, M.R. and Glen G. Glibert. 1996. College students' smoking behavior, perceived stress and coping styles. *Journal of Drug Education*, 26 (4): 367-76.

Nezu, A.M.1986. Effects of stress from current problems : comparison to major life events. *Journal of Clinical Psychology.* 42(6) : 847-852.

Norman, Tallent 1978. *Psychology of Adjustment.* Nastrand.

O'Mahony, J.F. and S.Hollwey. 1995. The correlates of being eaten in two nonpatient samples. *Addictive Behaviours.* 20(4) : 471-480.

Oswalt, R. and K. Silberg. 1995. Self-perceived Traumatic Stress in College : A survey. *Psychological Report.* 77(3) : pt.-1 : 985-1006.

Pahl, R.E. 1971. *Managers and Their Wives.* The Penguin Press, London.

Pearlin, Leonard I. 1989. Journal of Health and Social Behaviour. "The sociological study of stress.", 30: 241-56.

Pearlin, L.I. *et al.*1981. The stress process. *Journal of Health and Social Behaviour.* 22 : 337-356.

Pfeifer, S. and U.Waclty. 1995. Psychopathology and religious commitment : A controlled study. *Psychopathology.* 28(2) : 70-77.

Postgieter, J.R. and R.Venter. 1995. Relationship between adherence to exercise and scores on extraversion and neuroticism. *Peceptual and Motor Skills.* 81(2) : 520-522.

Quota, S. *et al.* 1995. The impact of the peace treaty on psychological well-being : A follow-up study of Palestinian Children. *Child Abuse and Neglect.* 19(10) 1197-1208.

Reed, M. and D. Derryberry. 1995. Temperament and response processing : Facilitatory negative consequence of positive and negative motivational states : *Journal of Research in Psychology.* 29(1) : 59-84.

Rees, L.1950. Body Size, Personality and Neurosis. *Journal of Mental Science.* 96.

Rehulkova, *et al.*1995. Adolescent's coping styles : A relation of the temperament. *Studia Psychological.* 37(3) : 159-161.

Reifman, A. and C. Dunckel - Schatter. 1990.Stress, Structural Social-Support, and well-being in University students. *Journal of American Coll. Health.* 38(6) : 271.

Roberts, S.M.1995. Applicability of the goodness-of-fit hypothesis to coping with daily hassles : *Psychological Report.* 77(3 pt.1) : 943-954.

Rohsenow, D.J. R.E. Smith, and S. Jahunso. 1985. Stress management training as a prevention programme for heavy social drinkers loguition, affect drinking and individual differences. *Addictive Behaviour.* 10(1). 45-54.

Rosen, E. Gregory, Ien.1965. *Abnormal Psychology.* London: W.B. Seunders Co.

Ruby, R.T. E.K.E. Gunderson, and R.E. Doll. 1969. Life stress and illness patterns in the U.S. Navy. *Archives of Environmental Health.* 19.

Ruiz– Caballero, J.A. and J.Bermudes. 1995. Neuroticism, mood and retrieval of negative personal memories. *Journal of General Psychology.* 122(1) : 29-35.

Sahni, Ashok (ed.) 1987. Health of the High Risk Groups: Mothers, Children and Eldeerly, Indian Society of Health administrators, Bangalore. 1987.

Sahni, Ashok (ed.) 1988. Health of Women and Children for Development, Indian Society of Health Administrators, Bangalore.

Sahni, Ashok (ed.) 1991.Health of the Youth and the Female Child. Indian Society of Health administrators, Bangalore.

Sahakian, Williams S. 1970. *Psychopathology Today: Experimentation, Theory and Research.* Chicago, Illinois, F.E. Peacock Publishers, 1970.

Saul, J.L.and J.Hovt. (eds.)1944. Physiological Effect of Emotional Tensions in J.Hovt. *Personality and the Behaviour Disorders.* Ronald Press.

Scheier, *et al.*1945. Distinguishing optimism from neuroticism and trait anxiety, self mastery, and self-esteem : A re-evaluation of the Life Orientation Test. *Journal of Personality and Social Psychology.* 67(6) : 1063-1078.

Scheier, T.H. and R.B.Cattell. 1961. *The Meaning and Management of Neuroticism and Anxiety.* New York : Ronald press.

Schutt, Russell K., Tatjana Meschede and Jill Rierdan. 1994. Distress, suicidal thoughts and social support among homeless adults. *Journal of Health and Social Behaviour,* 35: 134-42.

Selye, H. and C. Forlier (eds.)1950. Adaptive reactions to stress. In williams and Williams, *Life stress and Bodily Disease,* Baltimore.

Selye, H.1956. *The Stress of life.* New York : Mc Graw Hill.

Selye, H. 1976. *The Stress of Life* (revised edition). New York: McGraw-Hill.

Sheperd, *1967. A study at the University of California at Berkeley.*

Sharratt, G.1993. An analysis of occupational stress reported by Vietnam era veteran educators in Washington State. *Dissertation Abstract International.* 44(3).

Sinha, D. 1966. A Psychological analysis of some factors associated with success and failure in University education - intelligence, anxiety, and adjustment of achievers and non-achievers. *Psychological Studies.* 11(2) : 68-69.

Sullivan, R.1973. The Economics of Crimes : An Introduction to the Literature of Crime and Delinquency, *National Council on Crime and Delinquency.* 19(2) : 138.

Silva, Padmal. 1994. Post-traumatic stress disorder, cross-cultural Aspects. *International Review of Psychiatry.* 5 (2-3) : 217-229.

Spurrel *et al.* 1994. Post-traumatic stress disorder and coping after a natural disaster. *Social Psychiatry and Psychiatric Epidemiology.* 28(4) : 194-00.

Stagner, R.1974. *Psychology of Personality* New Delhi, (4th edition) : McGraw Hill Book Co.

Taylor, J.A. 1953. A personality Scale of Manifest Anxiety. *Journal of Abnormal Social Psychology.* 48 : 285-90.

Terry, W.S.1986. Caffeine and memory performance on the AVLT. *Journal of Clinical Psychology.* 42(6) : 860-703.

Torki, M.A. 1994. Associations between personality and stress reactions during and after invasion of Kuwait. *Psychological Report.* 74(2) : 667-673.

Vikem, R.L. *et al.* 1994. A development genetic analysis of adult personality : Extraversion and neuroticism from 18 to 59 years of age. *Journal of Personality and Social Psychology.* 66(4) : 722-730.

Vrana, S. and Lauterback,1994. Prevalence of traumatic psychological symptoms in a non-clinical sample of college student's. *Journal of Trauma Stress.* 7(2) : 189-302.

Walt, C.A. and R.L. Morris, 1995. The relationship among performance on a photic type indicators of perceptual defence/ vigilance, personality and extra sensory perception : *Personality and Individual Difference.* 19(5) : 635-648.

Wolf, H.G.1953. *Stress and Disease.* Thomas Spring Field. III.

Wolf, S. and H.Goodell and G. Wolf Harold.1968. *Stress and Disease* (2nd edition). Spring Field. III. Charles C. Thomas.

Wright, L.S.1985. Suicidal thuoghts and their family relationship to family stress and personal problem among high school seniors and college undergraduates. *Adolescence.* 20(79) : 575-80.

Zilboorg, G. and G.W. Henry 1941. *A History of Medical Psychology.* New York : Nortan.

Index

A

Academic Stress
Scales, 114-15, 150
In Arts/Science female college students, 130-31
In Upper/Lower class college girls, 149-50
In Higher/ Middle/Low economic levels, 160
In Post Graduate and Under Graduate college girls, 140
Academic achievement and personality, 96
Achievement Stress Scales
In Arts/Science female college students, 130-31
In Upper/Lower class college girls, 149
In Higher/Middle/Low economic levels, 159-60
In Post Graduate and Under Graduate college girls, 139
Adaptation
Syndrome, 29
Energy, 40
Adler, 86
Aggravating Factors of Stress, 21
Alarm reaction, 29
Alcohol consumption, 32
Allport, 86
Anxiety, 51, 86
Form, 52
Symptoms, 67
Approach avoidant conflict, 38
Arts/Science in Higher/ Middle/ Low Economic Groups, 167-68
Asthemic reaction, 52
Symptoms, 67
Atharva Veda, 22
And psychotherapy, 23
Attinson and Glass, 88
Auditory Verbal Learning Test, 87
Avila Study, 92

B

Bancroft et al study, 91
Bell Adjustment Inventory, 87

Berenbaum and Williams Study, 96
Bertollotti Study, 96
Bisht Battery of Stress Scales, 108-109, 127
Mean value of different aspects, 135
- in college students, 135
- in Post Graduate and Under Graduate, 147
- in Upper/Lower classes, 153
Body Clock, 30
Bonner and Rich Study, 80-81
Brain Power (diminished), 192
Breslan et al study, 100
Brown and Moskoitz Study, 101
Bulimia, 61
Byrne et al study, 97

C

Caffeine consumption, 32
Effect, 73, 92
Study, 87
Career choice and neurotic behaviour, 63
Caste demographics, 129
Caste-wise Comparison of Stress, 149
Causes of stress, 35
Chaudhary and Sinha, 87
Cigarette smoking effect of, 73
Cofer and Apley, 40
College stress (types), 44
Combat Exposure (CE) Symptoms, 94
Competition and stress, 22
Compulsive reaction, 55
Compulsions, 56
Concealed neurotic disorders, 63
Assessment, 64
Conclusions/hypothesis of study, 185, 202
Concentration (lack of), 52
Conflict, 37
Conversion
Disorder, 67
Reaction, 53
Coping ability, 75-76, 192
Coping strategy and personality, 98
Counselling services, 212
Current obsession in college girls, 189
Curriculum demographics, 128
Cysencle Personality Questionnaire, 100

D

Decline in grades, 193
Depression, 58
And menstrual cycle, 91
Depressive illness and personality traits, 95
Different Groups Mean Values on different MHQ aspects, 184

Dissociative Reaction, 54, 67
D'Lurilla and Sheedy Study, 77
Dopamine, 30-31
Double-approach/avoidant
  conflict, 38
Driskell and Olenstead study,
  83
Drug addiction, 62
DSM – III – R, 84
Duggun et al study, 95
Dynamics of stress, 35

E

Eating disorders, 61
Economic status demographics,
  129
Effects and signs of stress
  in girls, 188, 198
Emotional instability, 53
Empirical Approach, 111
Epstein and Katz Study, 75
Erin Brokovich case of positive
  impact of stress, 44
Exhaustion Stage, 29
Expectation from girls, 207
External frustration, 30
Extraversion and Neuroticism,
  90, 93, 95, 99
Extraversion-Neuroticism and
  Psychoticism (ENP), 98, 101
Eysenck's Two Dimensional
  Framework, 69
Eysenck Personality
  Inventory, (EPI), 87, 90, 92
  Questionnaire (EPQ), 94, 99

F

Families changes in, 22
Family Stress Scale, 118
Family stress
  In Arts/Science female
    College students, 136
  In Upper/Lower class
    college girls, 155
  In Higher/Middle/Low
    economic levels, 164
  In Post Graduate and
    Under Graduate college
    girls, 144
Federal Law in Mental Health
  Services, 195
Felsten's Study, 77
Fight or Flight response, 35
Findings of Study, 187, 196, 206
Five Factor Model (FFM), 95
Francis' Study, 89
Freud on neurosis, 86
Frustration, 36
Furneaux Factor, 89
Future uncertainty stress, 97

G

Garrison study, 81
Gender
  And stress relationship,
    209
  Specific programmes, 209-
    10
Gene Transposition, 33

Goodness of fit hypothesis, 76
Gotham, Sher and Wood study, 101
Gupta and Gupta study, 92

H

Happy messenger, 30
- Boosters, 31

Harris' study, 31
Health services for girl child, 211
High/Middle/Low economic levels comparisons in Different aspects of BBSS,163
- Mean values on different aspects of MHQ, 180-83

Hippocratic view of disease, 40
History of stress, 31
Hovonitz study, 74
Hypochondriasis, 61
Hypotheses of study, 185, 199, 204

I

Individual level changes, 212
Information Technology developments, 22
Inner pressure, 39
Internal frustration, 37
Introverts (neurotic), 94
Irmis study, 91
Israel-Palestine Peace Treaty impact on children, 98-99

J

Job security, 21
Jou and Fukada study, 82
Jung and Khalsa study, 75
Jung on neurosis, 86

L

Lepores' study, 78-79
Level of education demographics, 128
Life Orientation Test, 91
Limitations of study, 210
Loneliness, 58
Lynn and Martin study, 98, 101

M

Mac Dougal study, 73
Mackhan and Marris' study, 82
Maguns et al study, 87
Mangan et al study, 89
Manifest neurotic symptoms, 63
Marincola and Long study, 82
Mckenzie and Tindell study, 88
Mean values
- Of Arts and Science college girls on stress, 136-37
- Study conclusions, 138-39

Menstrual cycle complaints and depression, 91-92
Mental health problems, 194
Methodological Approach, 110
Middlesex Hospital Questionnaire (MHQ),108, 119-21

Mean comparison of Arts and Science students, 170
Different aspects, 172-74
Migraine, 27
And neuroticism, 100
Minugh and Harlow study, 73
Mobility in people, 22
Morris and Robinson study, 97
Murray et al study, 99
Mwamwenda study, 95
Myers et al study, 95
Myers Briggs Type Indicator (MBTI), 95

N

Neurosis
As disability, 62
Origin, 47
Scientific view, 70
Neurasthenia, 52
Neurotic depressive reaction, 57, 68
Neurotransmitters
Message sending, 30
Neurotic Behaviour, 46
Patterns, 47
Examples, 48
Symptoms, 49
- patterns, 51
Manifest symptoms, 63
Concealed disorders, 63
Assessment, 64
In young people
- therapy, 64
Famous people with, 66
Factors, 70
Concept, 85
Personality traits, 85
Nezu's study, 74
Novadrenalin, 30
Normative Approach, 113

O

Objectives of
Data analysis, 127
Investigation, 199
Obsessive compulsive reaction, 55, 68
Organic development, 55
Outer pressure, 39

P

People effected by stress, 36
Personal updating
- importance of, 213
Pfeifer and Waclty inventory, 93
Phobic reaction, 54
Phobias, 68
Physical Exercise and Yoga, 214
Physiological reaction of stress, 40
Physical Stress, 133, 142
Scales, 116-17
In Arts/Science female college students, 133
In Upper/Lower class college girls, 151

In Higher/Middle/low economic levels, 161
In Post Graduate and Under Graduate college girls, 142
Pituitary-adrenalin involvement, 40
Postgieter and Venter study, 99
Positive stress, 42
Post Traumatic Stress Disorder (PTSD), 76, 83-84
Pressures, 39
In college, 189-90
Present study, 103, 106
Aim, 106
Hypothesis, 106
Research design, 107
Procedure of tests, 124
Productive load, 75
Psychoneuro immunology, 194
Psychosomatic disorders, 22, 59
Effects, 59
Treatment, 22
Psychoneurotic disorders
- reaction, 67
Psychopathy, 49
Psychogenic amnesia, 54
Psychological reaction in stress, 40
Psychiatric field, 86
Psychological tests employed for collection of data, 108

Q

Quota et al study, 98
Quota for admissions, 211

R

Race and stress
- coping strategies, 75
Rational Approach, 111
Reed and Derryberry study, 94
Rehulkova et al study, 98
Rehabilitation principles, 65
Reifman and Dunken Schetter Study, 98
Results of stress, 30, 35
Risk taking bevaviours,195
Ruiz-Caballero and Bermudez study, 94

S

Sample of Study, 122-24, 200
Scheier and Cattell study, 85
Schizoids, 61
Seasonal Affective Disorder (SAD), and neuroticism, 99
Self Esteem (Low), 192
Selye's idea of systematic stress, 40
Sensory overload, 22
Serotonin, 30
Shastras in psychotherapy, 23
Silva study, 84
Sleep deprivation, 190-91
Smoking onset and stress, 97
Social acceptance of girl child, 211

Social environment and neurotic behaviour, 64
Social Stress Scales, 117-18, 134, 143
  In Arts/Science female college students, 134
  In Upper/Lower class college girls, 154
  In Higher/Middle/Low economic levels, 162
  In Post Graduate and Under Graduate college girls, 143
Social support, 78
  And stress, 75, 77
Somnambulism, 54
Somato-psychic disorders, 60
Spurrell study, 76, 84
State-Traity Anxiety Inventory, 94
Static Approach, 111
Stimulants craving, 191
Stress
  Concept, nature, word, 23-28, 71-72, 102
  Challenges, 28
  Symptoms, 28-29
  Syndrome effect, 30
  Reducers, 31
  Aggravants, 21
  History of, 32
  Studies, 74
  Concepts – relationship, 34
  Related illness, 209
Stressful situations
  - results of, 28
Stress-Distress Indicators, 34
Stress Management Training, 73
Substance use/Abuse factors, 73, 195
Sugar, 32
Suicide, 59
  In college students, 45
  - study, 45
  - factors, 59
Suicidal thought and stress-research, 79
Survival and stress, 32

T

Terry study, 87
Therapy, 65-66
Theoretical Approach, 111
Tobacco, 32
Torki study, 90
Total Stress
  In Arts/Science female college students, 137
  In Upper/Lower class college girls, 157
  In Higher/Middle/Low economic levels, 165
  In Post Graduate and Under Graduate college girls, 146
Transposable Elements (TE) insertions, 33

U

Unhealthy behaviours and stress,187

University of California study of
suicides, 45

V

Variables of study, 107-108
Measurement, 201
Vikem et al study, 90
Visuo Spatial Attention, 92
Vocational integration, 65
Vrana and Lauterbach study, 83

W

Walt and Morris study, 96
Wright's study, 79
On suicidal thoughts, 79

Y

Young adults Alcohol use
disorders (AUDs), 101